LINDA R. WAUGH

ROMAN JAKOBSON'S SCIENCE OF LANGUAGE

LISSE
THE PETER DE RIDDER PRESS
1976

ISBN 90 316 0112 8

Photoset in Malta by Interprint (Malta) Ltd.
Printed in The Netherlands by Intercontinental Graphics, Dordrecht

This work is dedicated
in admiration and friendship
TO ROMAN JAKOBSON
in celebration of his 80th birthday,
with deep appreciation of
his lasting and important contribution
to our understanding of
THE ESSENCE OF LANGUAGE

ACKNOWLEDGMENT

Professor Jakobson spent many hours with me giving me suggestions, comments, and criticisms of earlier versions of this work. I would like to thank him for his time and for the stimulus which his always incisive comments gave me.

TABLE OF CONTENTS

INTRODUCTION 7

I. SOME GENERAL NOTIONS 13
Relative Autonomy 13
Teleology 17
Relative Efficiency 18
Statics/Dynamics 20
Code/Message 23
Sound and Meaning 26
Selection/Combination (Similarity/Contiguity) 32

II. SPECIFICS OF STRUCTURE 37
Linguistic Sign 38
Structure: Relations 53
Structure: Part/Whole 56
Structure: Opposition 63
Relational Invariance 68
Markedness 89

CONCLUSION 101

BIBLIOGRAPHY 103

INDEX 110

INTRODUCTION

If one wanted to characterize Roman Jakobson's teachings on the nature of language,[1] it seems to me that they would best be described with the following adjectives: creative, original and imaginative, insightful and subtle, integrated, integrating and systematic, wide-ranging and consistent over time, over space, and over domains. What is perhaps most striking is the fact that while his teachings must be complex, because language is itself a complex entity, yet they are at the same time interwoven and interrelated by common threads, by certain overriding principles which, in his view, define the essence of language. It is the task of this monograph to sketch the outlines of his integrated point of view and at the same time to underscore those principles of organization which characterize language in general.

One of the most striking characteristics of Jakobson's work is the fact that while he has a highly consistent approach to all phenomena and has developed a coherent view of language structure, at the same time he is

[1]I would like to thank C. H. van Schooneveld for having first introduced me to Roman Jakobson's writings and for having instilled in me a respect for and an understanding of the essential insights contained therein. Many books, sections of books, articles, dissertations, etc. have been written about Jakobson or have acknowledged his inspiration almost since the beginning of his scholarly career. In the last ten years or so, one could cite Fischer-Jörgensen 1975, Holenstein 1974, 1975a, 1975b, Ivić 1965, Krámský 1974, Matejka 1975a, Malmberg 1970, Milewski 1964, Raible 1974, Rey 1974, Sangster 1970 (see the Bibliography), to name only those studies of his linguistic output which I have found to be most important. I have gained inspiration from all the works treating Jakobson, and while there is a certain amount of material which is common to them and to the present work, there is no complete overlap, since none has tried to show Jakobson's whole view of language, from a consistently linguistic point of view. With respect to the present manuscript, I would like to thank in particular the following, who were most helpful with comments and criticisms of earlier versions: Barbara Armstrong-Lafford, Dwight L. Bolinger, David Boruchowitz, Charles F. Hockett, Marcia Howden, James S. Noblitt, Frans van Coetsem. I have already acknowledged my great debt to Jakobson himself. I am also indebted to the Society for the Humanities, Cornell University, which generously supported the first preparation of this manuscript with a Faculty Summer Fellowship in 1975.

a subtle thinker who does not let the complexities of the particular object under study escape him. This makes my task difficult, for language is, as Jakobson himself has shown throughout his life's work, highly complex although unified — which means that the total conception to be presented here is highly complex although unified. At the same time, there is, behind the complexity and subtlety, an abiding belief that language may be simpler than we think, in the sense that the principles of organization, while subtle, are few and apply in certain interrelations throughout language. These principles may appear to be different in one domain as against another, but that is due to our own inability to seize on the constants and our failure to recognize the variations. There are invariants in the organizing principles of language; however, as will be discussed below, the invariants are never absolute, but relative to the system of which they are a part. I will then, to paraphrase Jakobson's "Retrospect" (1971a), be focussing on those constants which unify his inquiry into language, the invariance which is the keystone of his entire work.

Since the task I have set myself is such a large one, and cannot be completely fulfilled, especially in a monograph, I have made certain delimitations. Jakobson's total work covers more than just the science of language (as a glance at his *Selected Writings* will show) and at the same time many of the organizing principles of language to be discussed here are applicable to other domains (including the 'sciences of man') where language is an important consideration, as well as to the larger question of the relation between linguistics and biology, as the science of life.[2] I will, however, be concentrating first of all on Jakobson's view of the structure of language, and in particular his studies of phonology and grammar, although I shall touch upon (where appropriate) his work in historical linguistics, child language acquisition, aphasia, poetics, mythology, etc. Since there are certain overriding principles which define Jakobson's work, their application to the domains not covered should be obvious to the reader. Secondly, this work is presented as a summation of Jakobson's linguistic output in the last 60 years, based on a careful reading of that work and on personal communications with him. No attempt will be made to show the history of the development of his thought; this is basically a synchronic statement of his view as of the present moment. There are of course a few minor differences between his earlier and later works — he has kept developing throughout his scholarly career and is still developing. On the other hand, it is to

[2] See 1973e.

Jakobson's great merit (and see in this connection also van Schooneveld's dedication to 1971j) that he has been surprisingly consistent over those 60 years. On many things he has not changed his mind, but rather he has deepened his insight, made it more detailed and more specified, or perhaps applied it to a new domain. Again, his view of the principles of organization, of the essence of language has remained the same—what has developed is a full appreciation of those insights. Unfortunately, there is no time here to go into that development.

In a similar way, no systematic attempt will be made to show the convergence or divergence between Jakobson's view and that of the various thinkers who have influenced him the most: the Moscow School (Fortunatov — see 1971a, V–VII), the school of Baudouin de Courtenay and Kruszewski (see 1943, 454; 1970d; 1962g, 633); Husserl's phenomenology (1974d, 176; Holenstein 1974; 1975a; 1975b); Saussure and his school (for Saussure, 1962f; 1962g; 1967b; 1972c; 1972e; and for Sechehaye 1939d, 312); after Jakobson's arrival in America, Peirce (1966a, 346ff); and friendship and cooperation with N. S. Trubetzkoy (1939c; 1975g), Karcevskij (1956d), and Lévi-Strauss (1967b; 1972c; Mehta 1971; Lévi-Strauss 1976). Jakobson is a highly creative thinker who has read and digested a vast variety of work, studied and interpreted a number of languages, and done in some of these languages his own field work (especially in Slavic) — all of which has helped in developing his own science of language. He has consistently confronted his own ideas with those of other great scholars in linguistics (e.g. Saussure) and shares much with the linguistic tradition which he inherited; and he has been inspired by certain 'traditional' notions and by ideas developed by his contemporaries. But at the same time he has evolved a system which is highly original and perhaps even more radical and creative than some have thought. Some of the inspiration may have come from work by others (in linguistics and in related fields), but the interpretation of the inspiration and its integration into his overall view of language is Jakobson's own.

Many of the basic principles to be discussed here are, at the same time, part of the machinery of structuralism[3] in its various facets, and of 20th century (structural[4]) linguistics in particular. Structuralism was

[3]Structuralism has been defined as a methodology — but it is, in Jakobson's work, a methodology which has been derived from the object of study itself, and thus is at the same time a 'theory' of the intrinsic nature of that object of study. Given this, many of the principles to be discussed here are neither strictly 'theoretical' nor strictly 'methodological' — each is at the same time a statement about the nature of language, and about the way a student of language should approach his subject matter.

[4]'Structural' in the widest sense of the term (see 1973e).

outlined by Jakobson in ČIN, 1929, in the following way: "Any set of phenomena examined by contemporary science is treated not as a mechanical agglomeration but as a structural whole, and the basic task is to reveal the inner, whether static or developmental, laws of this system. What appears to be the focus of scientific preoccupations is no longer the outer stimulus, but the internal premises of the development; now the mechanical conception of processes yields to the question of their functions." (1973e, 11) So the fact that much of what is to be described here is part of the general notion of structuralism is not surprising, since Jakobson's work from the very beginning has been one of the driving forces of structuralism and, more particularly, of structural linguistics. In a certain sense we could say that his lasting and important impact on linguistics is the same as the advance that 20th century linguistics has made over previous centuries, since Jakobson's work has been most instrumental in defining linguistics as we know it. But what differentiates this scholar from other structuralists and from other linguists are those organizing principles he takes to be basic, the way in which they are interrelated, and their consistent and rigorous application in various domains. Thus, my task here is not to differentiate that which is originally Jakobson's and that which is not, but rather to show his total view of language. The whole, the essence of language according to Jakobson, is original; some of the parts may have been inspired by or influenced by other thinkers.

As to Jakobson's particular influence on linguistics, his work of course has had and continues to have a tremendous impact on the development of linguistic thought. And this with regard to both time and space factors. (It is sufficient to note, in order to appreciate the aspects of that influence, that his books, articles and papers have appeared in 19 different languages.) With respect to the future, it is the thesis of this monograph that his insight into language is extremely fruitful and productive; it has led to tremendous progress and insights in the past, and will, if properly understood and refined in the light of his own development, lead to progress and insights in the future, in those areas of linguistics which Jakobson himself has studied, those areas which he may not have investigated directly (there is almost nothing in linguistics proper which has not been at the very least indirectly touched by Jakobson's work), and those fields which join linguistics (i.e., the more encompassing domain of semiotic as well as the neighboring fields of psychology, sociology, cultural anthropology, etc.). But such development and full realization of the productive potential (productive in the linguistic sense of 'that which has a future') of his work depends on a deep appreciation of the principles of organization which he himself has discerned.[5]

Language is a system and consequently Jakobson's view of the essence of language is both a system and systematic. This means that the principles to be discussed here are all interwoven — none can be understood without appreciating its contribution to the larger whole and without recognizing the underlying unity of all of the principles. No system can be understood without knowing the whole, and in fact an understanding of any part of the system assumes that we know the whole beforehand. And this holds both for language and for Jakobson's thought. But, I must discuss the items one by one, in seriatim; the reader should keep in mind at all times that all these items (which themselves are sub-systems of the overall system) interact, and none can be understood without the others nor without the whole — and that is the important point about Jakobson's view of language. There is no simple way to proceed; one is perforce always jumping *in medias res*. I have, however, tried to draw a distinction between more general principles of linguistic structure (Part I) and more specific principles of linguistic structure (Part II), although at times the distinction is a hard one to draw and becomes arbitrary. But the overriding precept is still valid: a system can be appreciated as a system only when all the parts are known and seen in terms of their interrelationship to other parts and in terms of their contribution to the whole.[6]

[5]Since my task here is to present Jakobson's science of language so that it may be fully understood and in its own right, this work will provide no critique of his overall view nor of any specific facets of that view.

[6]Throughout this paper, I will be providing examples (in particular, from synchronic studies of phonology and grammar), of the various organizing principles of language. Specific references are given for examples that are Jakobson's own and for discussions which are inspired directly by a specific work. Otherwise, Jakobson's bibliography as a whole serves as a foundation for the discussion. The examples provided are not the only ones which could have been given; they are not important in and of themselves, but rather in the way they illustrate a given point. Furthermore, each example illustrates a given point in only one of its applications; in some cases diverse examples are provided to show the various facets of a particular point, but in no cases are all the ramifications explored. The examples thus provide only a framework for the understanding of the principle; they do not by any means exhaust the way in which the principle operates. In addition, the amount of space devoted to a given principle or to given examples does not necessarily reflect the amount of importance given to either the principle or the examples, but rather the amount of definition and explanation deemed necessary. With respect to terminology, I use Jakobson's term wherever possible; otherwise the terms were developed either by those who follow his view or by Jakobson himself in discussing this manuscript.

PART I

SOME GENERAL NOTIONS

RELATIVE AUTONOMY

According to Jakobson, language is a structured, relatively autonomous entity which first of all exists 'in and of itself' and which second of all is integrated into the larger framework of human endeavors and characteristics. Language has its own integrity and specific nature, which is not reducible to, nor deducible from other entities, no matter how closely related. Yet at the same time, it does not exist in complete isolation from other domains, and the limits between language and other objects of study are not absolute ones. It is not at all the case, for example, that language is one thing and culture or the physical make-up of the brain are completely different things, unrelated to language.

The principle of RELATIVE AUTONOMY[1] (AUTONOMY IMPLYING INTEGRATION) means that one should not bring, e.g., a priori physical, psychological, biological, logical, philosophical, etc. constructs or concepts nor an a priori methodology or evaluative measure, to the study of language. All of these must come from language itself. We bring, of course, our accumulated experience in other domains, but we must not, arbitrarily, impose anything from those domains which may be contradicted in the object of study. Furthermore, language is different from, but related to, society, culture, the brain, consciousness, etc. and any 'cooperative' venture to relate them should not assume a simplistic equivalence between them. But at the same time, no one who studies language should isolate it from those domains with which it has an obvious relationship — the study of language as if it were not, e.g., a part of culture is equally fallacious, for no real understanding of the

[1] Autonomy with (or implying) integration and relative autonomy are favorite elements of Jakobson's terminology. See 1960a; 1971a, 711, 716; 1971b, 182, 317, 594–5, 706; 1973e; as well as Matejka 1975a.

nature of language can be had, if we forget that it is an integral and integrating part of culture. So language must be studied as it is without imposing principles from other domains and without, at the same time, arbitrarily divorcing it from the larger context into which it is integrated. The study of language assumes at the same time a larger study where the "common foundations and developmental lines as well as the mutual dependence" (1973e, 26) of language and other domains is emphasized. But there is a methodological priority: Jakobson insists "on the pre-eminent importance of an immanent analysis which locates itself within the work. Only after the function and structure of the work itself have been studied should the more traditional tasks of relating it to history or psychology or of establishing its connections with other disciplines or with the world be undertaken." (de George, 1972, xxii) On the other hand, Jakobson firmly believes now that "we are faced with an urgent need for interdisciplinary teamwork to be pursued diligently by savants of different branches." (1973e, 25)

This principle applies to language itself in terms of its definition and to its component parts. Thus, claims Jakobson, "criteria peculiar to technical constructs are imposed arbitrarily upon natural languages not only by logicians but sometimes also by linguists themselves. For example, we run up against heteronomous and forced attempts to reduce natural language to declarative statements and to view requisitive (interrogative and imperative) forms as alterations or paraphrases of declarative propositions." (1973e, 30) All elements of language (either in the sense of parts like the phonemic system or in the sense of units like the morpheme or in the sense of coded material like the 'accusative case' or '/n/' or 'interrogative particle' or in the sense of coded matrices like the preposition + object construction) come from the structure of language itself and are not assumed to exist because of their reality in other, even though related, domains or because of their basis in linguistic tradition. Furthermore, if an element of language is assumed to exist, it is not necessary that an operational definition of that unit be given — it is enough to show first of all the relatively automous nature of the unit in the overall system.

Thus, each part is (relatively) autonomous in that it has its own place in the overall pattern; but at the same time, since it does belong to an overall whole, its *raison d'être* comes from its integration into that overall whole. Thus, for example, written language (as against spoken language) or the poetic use of language (as against ordinary speech), while they may be autonomous and may necessarily contain certain regulating characteristics peculiar to their own nature, are both integrated into the overall pattern of language. Similarly, child language and the developing patterns of speech in the infant learning a language, as well as aphasic loss, have certain properties peculiar to their status *vis-à-vis* normal adult language. There is neither an isomorphic relation between them nor an unbridgeable chasm. There are certain similarities between the build-up of a child's phonemic system and the hierarchy of distinctive features operative in the adult system — but there are differences also (e.g., in Russian, palatalized dentals are learned before non-palatalized ones, and yet in the system of Russian the palatalized consonants are clearly the secondary, marked ones (1941, 78)); these differences do not invalidate the relationship between the two, but show that a mechanical assumption of identity is naïve and unsupported. The child's learning of a language is a relatively autonomous patterning.

Furthermore, the relative autonomy of the input pattern accounts for the difference between encoder and decoder (alias speaker and hearer, writer and reader) and between the active and passive knowledge of grammar, and for the prior passive knowledge of a language by children and adults. Not only are competence and performance relatively autonomous in relation to each other, but competence itself is subdivided into, e.g., the relatively autonomous competences in dialogues and monologues (1968c).

It is also in this sense of autonomy that Jakobson envisions a (relatively) autonomous phonology. First of all, the distinctive features and the phonemes as their bundles are in his view units of linguistic reality — and not theoretical or extrinsic constructs. The distinctive features are 'distinctive' in terms of the linguistic system; how they are psychologically relevant remains for future research. Certainly, it is the case that for perception speakers rely on the redundant, configurative, and expressive features as well. Furthermore, as Jakobson himself has said, the distinctive features are not the only (perceptually) pertinent ones, but they are the primary pertinent[2] ones in the explicit code.

Furthermore, phonology has its own internal organization and coherence, due on the one hand to its unique place in the system of language and on the other hand to its relations with the other (relatively

[2]It is for this reason that Jakobson has objected to the translation *trait pertinent* in French for *distinctive feature*.

autonomous) parts of language. Phonology then is different from but related to e.g., morphology and syntax, and conversely, morphology and syntax are different from but related to phonology (1949e; 1962e)[3]. Given this, one should not study phonology in isolation from these other domains, but in terms of the similarities and differences between them. That is, one expects phonology to share certain principles of organization with these other parts of language while at the same time it will have other principles of structuring unique to itself.

Likewise, there is in Jakobson's view a major difference between the WORD level (the largest coded units) and the phrase, clause, sentence levels (coded MATRICES[4]) —in their interrelation both are relatively autonomous domains. But "the difference between the word level and the sentence level is, however, no iron curtain. Limitations must be made between problems, but they are never to be absolute limits as if the sentence is one thing and the word is another. It must be kept in mind that the differences are rather differences of relation, of hierarchy, and not differences which can be determined by false and absolute definitions." (1972b, 34)

Furthermore, language is, in Jakobson's view, characterized by a set of antinomies (to be defined later): dynamic/static, diachronic/ synchronic, archaic/newfangled, ellipsis/explicitness, metaphor/metonymy, concurrence/sequence, similarity/contiguity, selection/combination, code/message, speech event/narrated event, homogeneity/ individuation, free/patterned, particular/universal, encoder/decoder, signans/signatum, independent/redundant, lexical meaning/grammatical meaning, invariance/variation, equivalence/difference, overall/ contextual, distinctive/conceptual, intrinsic/contextual, marked/unmarked (for some of these see 1956b, 243, and 1975f, 5), where the members of each pair are relatively autonomous *vis-à-vis* each other but at the same time integrated into a larger whole (their synthesis). In fact, the 'dialectic tension' in the opposites within each pair of the antinomies is only resolved through their integration.

[3] Jakobson has insisted upon this from the very beginning: "M. Jakobson fait remarquer que la phonologie n'est pas une partie de la grammaire, mais une branche spéciale de la linguistique à côté de la grammaire. La grammaire s'occupe des symboles et la phonologie des parties composant ces symboles. Le fait qu'il y a des cas où un phonème en lui-même fait fonction de symbole, n'est pas en contradiction avec cette différence en principe. C'est le morphème qui est l'élément le plus petit en grammaire." (1931, 297)

[4] Coded matrices are defined on page 49.

TELEOLOGY

Language, according to Jakobson, is not solely a material entity, although it uses sound material as its primary means of expression, for the end which language serves is not a material one, and the means which language uses is not equal to its function. This is a classic example of a semiotic entity: the use of a physical medium to communicate something different from, but associated with, that physical medium. The material is given only as a means of transfer to the meaning — it is matter which transfers something else. The matter is only a means to an end — communication of meaning.

To elaborate, in Jakobson's view, with respect to a semiotic entity, one can understand neither the entity itself nor any given part of it nor any changes which might take place within the entity without asking the fundamental question: why does it exist? What end does it serve? What is its function? With respect to the TELEOLOGY of language (a teleology of ends, of goals and of the means used for these ends, not of final causes — see 1963c, 1975c), Jakobson's answer has always been clear-cut and unequivocal: language serves an inter- and intra-personal[5] communicative function, and its intrinsic aspects are based on that fact. Again, one may say, paraphrasing Erlich (1955, 198) who in turn was paraphrasing Jakobson (1933–34), that the "communicative function is neither the only pertinent aspect of language nor merely one of its components, but a strategic property informing and permeating the entire structure, the principle of dynamic integration, or, to use a key term of modern psychology, a *Gestaltqualität*".

Language is an inter- and intra-personal (inter- and intra-subjective in another terminology) TOOL for verbal communication and cognition. The inherent nature of language itself and of each and every one of its parts and the changes which languages undergo, are definable only with respect to this overriding criterion. This means, most particularly, that every part of language plays a role with respect to this communicative function; no part is arbitrary in the sense that it has no communicative role to play. Thus, for example, on the one hand, written language, the elliptical sub-code, dialoguical competence, various language changes, or on the other hand, inner speech, the phoneme,

[5]The dialogue is not confined to the intra-personal form of communication but involves also internal speech, discussion with oneself, intracognitive communication. It may of course be highly elliptical, but is nonetheless linguistically based.

the syllable, the word as well as the cases in Russian, the derivational suffix-*ka* in Russian, the particle *by* in Russian, have a purpose. In fact, in language, all differences have their function.

With respect to the problem of teleology, Jakobson has often pointed out that the reason for the existence of given forms in language is "not to figure in certain given constellations" (1949g, 38) (i.e., to have a given distribution or to find their essence in certain concurrent or sequential combinations) but rather to signify, to serve communication. Thus, in his famous discussion (1971a, 639) of the 'dining car', Jakobson claims that in order to know what a 'dining car' is, we must know what its function is. And furthermore, in order to relate it to its context, we must know what the function of the context is. And if the 'cars' are different, then their aim is different. And that difference is relevant. This lesson is nowhere more important than in the study of syntax, for it is here that we are dealing most clearly with the constellations, the sequential combinations. There is a tendency in some studies of syntax to equate the reason for the existence of these constellations with their very existence. But, in addition to being a vicious circle, it should be clear that Jakobson's warning should be heeded here as elsewhere—the constellations occur because they have a signifying function to fulfill. No study of syntax will understand its object fully if this significative function is not kept in mind at all moments of the analysis. As Jakobson's analysis of such grammatical categories as gender, number, and case has shown, a non-significative study of such categories robs them of their *raison d'être* and leads the investigator to make conclusions about their nature which become nonsensical when viewed from the functional point of view. In like fashion, language changes are not blind, fortuitous, arbitrary — but goal-directed in the sense that there is always a reason for language change and that reason can be analyzed (e.g., the change may serve to correct an imbalance in the system and thereby may establish a new structural patterning).

RELATIVE EFFICIENCY

The notion of imbalance as well as the notion of change point to another facet of language — its RELATIVE EFFICIENCY. To say that language is efficient is to say that in general its patterning is such that communication may take place — but while the linguistic system is in general an efficient one (else how could human beings learn and use such a complex pattern?) it also is clear from the study of language itself as well as from language change, that the system is in certain respects not maximally efficient (or maximally simple or economical). Language is efficient — or else it would not survive and would be replaced by other, more efficient systems. The efficiency of language is the efficiency of the overall system, thus implying the relative efficiency of the component parts in terms of each other. However, there is an interrelation between the parts of the system and the lack of any absolute balance between different functions, as in any social system. Efficiency need not imply a razor-edged simplicity. In fact, efficiency in one area (i.e., a small number of features and their combinations into phonemes and sequences) may lead to non-efficiency in another area (i.e., a large number of homonyms or of long words). Efficiency in morphology or in the number of words may lead to longer or more intricate syntactic constructions. There is always a trade-off. It is, in essence, a question of hierarchy. The hierarchy of the units from the largest to the smallest is diverse. Furthermore, the economy of one level is accompanied by lesser economy of other levels. Furthermore, 'holes' may occur in the system — the language may have a /k/ but no /g/ and yet have the related /p/, /b/, /t/, and /d/. And there is no reason to suppose, for instance, particularly in the lexicon, that all logical combinations of all lexical features will occur. The Latin deponent verbs lack 'active' counterparts and yet do not lose, by virtue of that, their passive (grammatical) marking. Furthermore, in the Russian case system, the genitive in *-u* and locative in *-ú* are not efficiently used in comparison with their counterparts (genitive in *-a*, locative in *-e*). Thus, some parts of the language pattern may be more economical (or more simple) than other parts — and in no way should the analyst impose economy there where it does not exist.

Perhaps one of the most important aspects of the 'relative' nature of efficiency is the efficiency (economy) of the overall system, which leads to the reduction of REDUNDANCY, as against the highly redundant nature of certain coded units as well as of language use. Given the fact that language is used for communication and that in terms of perception, communication is, up to a point, more efficient when more redundant, the whole pattern of language as well as of its component parts is redundant. The analyst may reduce redundancy in terms of revealing the 'bare bones' of the phonological and grammatical systems, but such reduction does not mean that the redundancies are not pertinent for perception (in fact they are, in those terms, highly pertinent — 1968a) nor does it mean that the redundancies are not important in terms of the system itself. Redundancy is part of the system — and the organization of redundant elements is part of the system.

STATICS/DYNAMICS

With respect to the opposition of STATICS and DYNAMICS, for Jakobson synchronic structure does not imply statics. There is statics in both DIACHRONY (that which has not changed over a certain period of time — relational invariance on the temporal axis) and SYNCHRONY (that which does not seem to be changing at a given moment) while there is dynamics in both diachrony (accomplished, completed language change) and synchrony (changes in progress at a given moment, as well as language creativity and productivity). Change is both a synchronic and a diachronic fact. A given synchronic state, then, will always have the remains of past changes and the beginnings of future changes built into its structure. And, in fact, it is the built-in potential for change without collapsing which differentiates language from other systems.[6] The time axis is part and parcel of the linguistic system. Thus, for example, the opposition between the explicit and elliptical sub-codes may carry the additional marking of an old-fashioned variant (in the explicit sub-code) as against a new-fashioned variant (in the elliptical sub-code). The two are not equal in terms of their role in the system. In like fashion, so-called 'free variation' normally carries a stylistic difference, which may again reflect a change in progress. In phonology, given the distinctive meaning of the phonological distinctive features, the difference between the two variants may be a stylistic one (e.g., unreleased $[p^{\urcorner}]$ vs. released, aspirated $[p^h]$ in word-final position in English) reflecting as well the difference between explicit and elliptical sub-codes. In semantics, the stylistic differences may be an overlay to the different conceptual markings of the particular units. Such stylistic differences give a 'free' choice to the speaker, require a selection on his part; his selection is, however, dictated by the emotive or emphatic role the units play. Furthermore, the difference between the basic, central variant (*Grundbedeutung*) and peripheral, contextual variants of a grammatical or

[6]In this way, language is essentially different from a motor: in a motor there can be dynamics in the sense of movement; in language there is movement and change, where change can actually evidence its creative and productive potential.

lexical item may reflect changes in progress or may be the result of past changes. Such concepts, (some of which will be discussed later), as the relation between marked and unmarked, the hierarchy of central and peripheral variants, the problem of stylistic variation, the relationships and natures of the sub-codes, the changing shape of the code as a child learns it, the nature of the idiolect of one individual over time, the reversible vs. irreversible aspects of time, i.e., the differentiation, then partial merger, and then rehabilitated differentiation of /ã/ and /õ/ in French vs. the differentiation, then complete merger of /ɛ̃/ and /œ̃/ in French (1949d), the changing character of an individual's mastery over the overall code, etc. must be understood in the light of the dynamic nature of language.

LANGUAGE CHANGE is, for Jakobson, a recoding, a restructuring (see 1949a). Thus, according to him, we must understand the structure before the change begins, the structure after it takes place, the sense of the change undergone in respect to the undergoing system, the level at which the change takes place (e.g., distinctive feature or phoneme), the effects of the change on the system.[7] This last is particularly important, for no change can bring about a typologically impossible synchronic state. Change, whether internally or externally motivated, is goal-directed, either on a subliminal or on a conscious level; but we cannot, at the moment, discover final causes, nor can we predict with absolute certainty ultimate ends. However, we can detect and interpret the general tendencies of changes without being able to predict the final results absolutely: certain types of patterning are impossible, certain other types contain particular implications, certain others are more favored statistically. And so forth. It is clear that although a knowledge of synchrony is absolutely essential for understanding language change, the fact that a given structure is the product of past changes and harbors within it future changes, requires an ever-present awareness on the part of the linguist and an ever-present (even if subconscious) awareness on the part of the members of the speech community of the MUTABILITY of language, for it clearly is one of the organizing principles of language. Furthermore, changes show what has a future and what does not in terms of a given system. And here we enter the realm of PRODUCTIVITY, for that which is productive is that which has

[7]Here, of course, as in the distinction between diachrony and synchrony and dynamics and statics, Jakobson diverges widely from Saussure. Saussure saw no systematicity in change.

a future at the given moment. But again, productivity can be reversed — e.g., certain irregular conjugations of verbs, which seem to be limited to a small class of verbs, may suddenly attain a 'productive status' and be used as the standard of new words.

The dynamic character of language is not only temporal, it is also SPATIAL; spatial invariance and spatial difference as well as changes in an overall code on a spatial basis are also inherent to the structure of language. In addition to the evident fact that dialect differences must be understood with reference to the system of which they are a part, and not treated atomistically and non-functionally, the expansion of change over space must be rigorously studied in terms not only of differences in a given system but also of convergence between systems (the so-called *Sprachbund* or 'linguistic affinity' problem — see 1949b) and the creation of pidgins and creoles.

But perhaps the most important aspect of the dynamic nature of language is its CREATIVITY. Not only is it the case that every individual has a variety of sub-codes at his disposal, for use in different situations, and which he can creatively alter as new situations arise, but also and more importantly, the creativity of language is seen in the new combinations which any speaker can make (phrases, clauses, sentences, utterances, discourses) including the creation of new linguistic and extralinguistic contexts for old words. Nowhere does this show up more intensely than in the poetic use of language[8] and in metaphoric and metonymic constructions. The poet, rather than creating deviant contexts, utilizes the creative aspect of language to its fullest. This creative aspect of language depends on the whole structure of language itself — or, one could say, the whole structure of language is designed in such a way as to provide creativity (or freedom) in terms of higher-level structures (phrases, sentences, etc.) while allowing very little freedom in terms of lower-level structures (phonemes, syllables, words). Moreover, as we ascend the hierarchy of linguistic units (phoneme, syllable, morpheme, word, phrase, clause, sentence, utterance, a set of sentences spoken by one speaker, discourse, an exchange of utterances by two or more speakers) the freedom to create novel contexts increases. And of course, this most important facet of the creativity of language — poetic creations — is also based on the fact that neither language nor any of its component parts is a material entity.

[8]This point has also been made in an unfinished manuscript by R. B. Sangster on the interrelation of Jakobson's work in poetics and in linguistics.

CODE/MESSAGE

The non-material nature of language has even farther-reaching implications. In terms of the semiotic, non-material nature of the whole, we have the antinomy and means-ends relation between CODE and MESSAGE, where message is defined by Jakobson as the unique, semelfactive, single act of speech, while the code is the system (the nature of which is to be described herein) which underlies and makes possible that and every other message. Code then is not a material entity, but rather a semiotic one, which requires at the same time the collective consensus of the individual speakers and is in this sense akin to folklore (which requires also collective consensus for its existence) but different from literature (which can exist without such consensus). But the antinomy of code and message for Jakobson is not, as it was for Saussure, social vs. individual. On the one hand everyone has his personal code, which is used in particular for inner speech; and on the other hand various messages reflect different degrees of socialization. In interpersonal communication, the encoder may (consciously or unconsciously) adapt his own personal code closer to that of his interlocutor in order for communication to take place. Thus, while the relative autonomy of the idiolect *vis-à-vis* the code may be discernible, yet it must be integrated into a more general, shared code for communication to take place.

Jakobson has also insisted on the fact that the code is not a monolith: it is made up of (relatively autonomous) SUB-CODES dependent on the different roles and radiuses of communication of the speaker. The code is not static but dynamic, a diversified, convertible code, with differentiations as to functions and as to time and space factors. This is shown for example in the different stages between elliptic and explicit communication and in the different social and spatial dialects which all speakers exhibit. And of course, ELLIPSIS plays an enormous role in language change: it is in the differentiation of elliptical vs. explicit sub-codes that the dynamic nature of language is especially apparent. There is then no monolithic unity of code; but there is a unity of sub-codes in that they all depend upon one another for the differentiation of their applications and functions and in that they overlap in certain definable ways.

But to differentiate the code from the message is not to divorce them completely. In fact, as Jakobson has pointed out, "the variety of virtual messages" (1973e, 24) is restricted by the structural laws inherent to any given code. Furthermore, one of the most important of Jakobson's discoveries about the structure of language comes from his work on the various categories of language built on the relationship between code and message. In fact he distinguishes 4 types of relationship depending on the relation between code and message (1957a):

I. Circularity

M/M Message referring to message. Reported speech, quoted speech, quasi-quoted speech, etc.;

C/C Code referring to code. Proper names (for the general meaning of a proper name is that the name has been assigned to a given individual): "the name means anyone to whom this name is assigned" (1957a, 131).

II. Overlapping

M/C Message referring to code. Metalinguistic usage, definitions, etc.

C/M Code referring to message, in which the general meaning "cannot be defined without a reference to the message" (1957a, 131).

This last-mentioned category is that of 'SHIFTERS' or (using Peirce's terminology) indexical symbols, and brings forth one of the most important problems of linguistic structure studied by Jakobson — that of deixis. Examples of 'shifters' include (in the Russian verb) person, mood, tense (1957a; 1966a).

Shifters also show the importance of the SPEECH EVENT for the categorization in language. Deictic categories depend, for the interpretation of their meaning, upon the speech event in which they are uttered — or, to put it differently, they all subcategorize in some way the speech event (the speech event is, after all, one part of the world of human experience about which we speak) and hence the speech event itself enters into the meaning of many linguistic categories. The speech event is most important for the differentiation of deictic categories not only with respect to the relationship encoder–decoder (giving person in all languages and gender in some) but also for grammatical categories (e.g., tense, and mood) as well as many lexical ones (e.g., *come*, *today*, *tomorrow*, *this*, etc.). Deixis, in particular, is built on the dialectic tension between code and message, on the anticipation of the message within the code and on the antinomy of the narrated event and speech event, on the interconnection of the narrated event and the speech event. Thus, while every meaning category exists in the code, it is implemented always in the message: in deictic elements, however, this implementation is played upon in the very definition of the meaning. Furthermore, in order for an addressee to understand the use of a given form in a given message, he must take into account the fact of the transmission of the message (the use of the message in a given speech situation[9]). Deixis is obviously one of the most important facets of linguistic structure.

But it should be pointed out, here as elsewhere, that the speech event itself relates to various functions of language. Jakobson has recognized six linguistically relevant facets of the SPEECH EVENT (1960a):

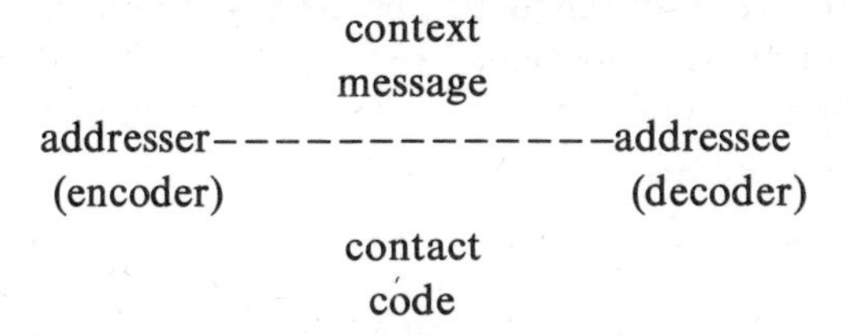

It is on the basis of these six facets that he differentiates the six relevant FUNCTIONS of language depending on the set (or focus or orientation: *Einstellung*) of the speaker toward one of the six facets of the speech event:

referential (ideational)
poetic
emotive conative
phatic
metalinguistic

The emotive function is exemplified by interjections and by the stylistic use of long vowels for emphasis in English; the conative function is exemplified by vocatives and imperatives; the referential (or ideational) function is exemplified by the majority of messages informing about the outside world or our ideas; the phatic function is exemplified by queries as to whether contact is still maintained ('can you hear me?'); the metalinguistic function is exemplified by language dealing with language (discussed earlier in connection with shifters: C/C): and the poetic function is exemplified with particular intensity by poetry. It is of course

[9] It has been postulated (van Schooneveld MS) that deixis may well be the most important integrating factor of the semantic system, and that the reference to the speech situation within the code may be much more wide-spread than is currently thought, that meaning in particular is essentially and inherently built on the notion of deixis.

poetic usage, the productivity and creativity inherent in poetic usage as well as the focus on the linguistic material itself, which has had a profound effect upon Jakobson's whole view of language.

The speech event is also important for the antinomy encoder/decoder. Generally speaking, one's competence as a decoder is higher than one's competence as an encoder. Furthermore, questions of ambiguity become quite different when viewed from the point of view of the encoder and when viewed from that of the decoder. Moreover, the differentiaion of various subcodes (dialects) as well as the definition of inner speech reside in the relationship speaker/addressee. Most importantly, the teleology of language and its communicative function find their basis in the speech event: "we speak to be heard and need to be heard in order to be understood" (1971i, 47) and the whole structure of language is built on this evident fact.

SOUND AND MEANING

Sound

Another conclusion from the fact that language is a semiotic entity is that PHONOLOGY is in this view concerned not only with the sound material of language, but more importantly, with the end which this sound material serves with respect to the communicative function of language. Phonemes and distinctive features are not strictly material entities, even though their means of expression is material:

> sound matter in language [is] neither divorced from the actual physical properties of the speech signal nor entirely reducible to a purely physical analysis of sound, whether in its acoustic or physiological aspects ... One cannot afford, therefore, either to isolate the functional aspect of sound structure from its material support, nor [sic] to study the physical properties of sounds apart from their purely linguistic (i.e. semantic) function. This is the essence of relative autonomy at the level of phonology. (Sangster, 1970, 124)

Phonemes and distinctive features are goal-directed entities always. This is especially clear if one considers that for the hearer of a given linguistic message the 'reality' with which he is concerned is neither the acoustic spectrum nor the articulatory movements of the speaker nor the nerve impulses to the brain, but rather the FUNCTION of the sounds in the given linguistic system. His focus is on perceiving them in order to understand what the speaker has said, and any question of perception is necessarily linguistic, because perception is necessarily carried out with respect to the linguistic nature of the sounds themselves. This means first of all that speech sounds are perceived differently from other sounds, and evidence for the special character of speech as against other sounds frequently cited by Jakobson comes from experimentation, especially the specialization of certain parts of the brain for speech, as well as from the categorial perception of speech sounds by speakers of a given language as against the not necessarily categorial perception of other sounds (1973e, 1972a). Secondly, this means that any discussion of the production of sounds and of the acoustico-motor (physical) effect of sounds without taking into account their linguistic nature is an empty exercise. PHONETICS should not and cannot be a non-linguistic (i.e. strictly physical) study of sound but rather a study which analyzes their physical attributes keeping in mind always their functional attributes. In effect, (speech) sound *per se*, according to Jakobson, does not exist outside of language — all in sound is linguistic. In this respect, Jakobson professes a linguistic imperialism. The vocal apparatus is the way it is and functions the way it does because of its use for language. Non-linguistic sounds — such as coughs, etc. — are, says Jakobson in agreement with Thomas Aquinas (1970d, 395–6), *ad hoc* and secondary productions of the speech mechanism. The divorce of speech sounds from the 'gross acoustic sound matter' is an artificial one — the gross acoustic sound matter exists only because of its function in the linguistic system: speech sounds are units made for use in language. (Here we see again his means-ends view of language.) Sound is, according to Jakobson, again in agreement with Thomas Aquinas, artificially prepared for language. And the phoneme and the distinctive features literally occur and are literally perceived in the sound matter. And while

> Phonemes draw on the sound matter but readjust this extrinsic matter, selecting, dissecting, classifying it along their own lines. These items of sound matter are transformed into semiotic elements. (1949g, 36–7)

it is also the case that 'extrinsic' stuff would not exist except in so far as it is used for the linguistic system. In fact, then, it is only extrinsic at first glance — it is really intrinsic to the linguistic system through the value set upon it by that system and through its participation in the system. Thus, an overriding 'empiricism' with respect to speech sounds is, for Jakobson, non-empirical, and the semiotic study of speech sounds becomes the 'empirical' discipline, for a strictly physical study of speech sounds treats neither their inherent nature nor their integration into a linguistic system.

Meaning

In much the same way MEANING (*signatum*) in language is not a material entity, but part of the linguistic system, and the 'closed universe' characteristic of the speech sounds is also the case for (linguistic) meaning. At a first, superficial glance, it seems that Jakobson has always contended, following a venerable tradition, that meaning is to be consistently and rigorously separated from its 'material' support — REFERENCE (*denotatum*) or ontological reality. Reference is extra-linguistic and referential items may have a reality of their own, but the question of their semiotic status within a linguistic system remains unanswered without a rigorous and consistent attempt to show the role they play with respect to the communicative function of language. This of course is the philosophical notion of the difference between meaning and reference, of the imposition of a linguistic classification or categorization upon extra-linguistic reality, and one which is supported by many diverse facts (see 1944; 1953c; 1959a; 1959d). The phrases 'that bottle is half-empty' and 'that bottle is half full' may refer to the same entity but show the difference in the frame of reference of the speaker: whether he compares the given situation with a full bottle or an empty bottle. They may also brand him as a pessimist or an optimist. The phrases 'quarter to 3', 'fifteen minutes to 3', '45 minutes after 2', '2:45' (examples used by Jakobson in 1972b and in personal discussion) all exist but they may reflect a prospective vs. retrospective frame of reference on the one hand and the desire for more vs. less precision on the other. The sentences 'the secretary arrived with the minister' vs. 'the minister arrived with the secretary', 'Latvia is bordered by Estonia' vs. 'Estonia is bordered by Latvia' (1936), 'Eisenhower and Krushchev' vs. 'Krushchev and Eisenhower' reflect the hierarchy of importance attached by the speaker to the two different items. The active and the passive ('natives hunt lions' vs. 'lions are hunted by natives', 1972a) reflect a difference in focussing; furthermore, in the latter the agent of the hunting can be omitted ('lions are hunted'). 'Morning star' and 'evening star' are different chronometric and astronometric designations of the same entity — the planet Venus. Moreover, we can talk about non-existent entities or entities whose existence may not be directly observable: 'unicorn', 'ambrosia', 'nectar', 'gods', 'angels' (1959a) as well as abstract concepts which have no clear referent: 'happiness', 'freedom', 'peace', 'but', 'if', 'with'. 'Colorless green ideas sleep furiously', 'John doesn't play golf: golf plays John' (1959d) both express concepts which are linguistically relevant. As Jakobson has pointed out, "the non-existence, the fictitiousness of these entities has no bearing on the question of their semantic significance. The possibility of questioning their being is the best warning against a confusion of ontological irreality with senselessness." (1959d, 495).

And in fact it is Jakobson's contention that we can never know the meaning of a word in a given linguistic system by acquaintance with the referents of that word. This is obviously so in the case of words which have no referents, for it is only through a linguistic acquaintance with the linguistic terms that we understand these words; but it also is so in the case of words with a seemingly obvious referent. For example, "no one can understand the word *cheese* unless he has an acquaintance with the meaning assigned to this word in the lexical code of English. . . . nobody has ever smelled or tasted the meaning of *cheese*. . . . The meaning of the word "cheese" cannot be inferred from a nonlinguistic acquaintance with cheddar or with camembert without the assistance of the verbal code." (1959a, 260)[10] We can know the meaning of *cheese* only through verbal explanation in the same language or another language (1953c; 1959a). Moreover, although we do utter speech sounds, we do not go around carrying referents on our backs (1953c) as a means of communicating the meanings. Meanings are 'intelligible, mental, conceptual, translatable' but not directly perceivable, neither in sound nor in the outside world.

As a consequence of observations such as these, Jakobson has recently (see 1972b) gone much further and views the dichotomy of *signatum* vs. *denotatum* as naïve and unsupported. Reference may be extra-linguistic, but when we speak it becomes linguistic: it is linguistic, it has a linguistic aspect. And it is this linguistic aspect which is of relevance. If we go back to the examples 'morning star' and 'evening star', the referents are not the same, in that we as human beings experience

[10]Furthermore, despite seeming similarities, English *cheese* and Russian *syr* are slightly different. *Syr* is limited to fermented curd of milk; *cheese* is not. Thus, *cottage cheese* is translated by *tvorog* in Russian (1959a, 261).

them in two different temporal dimensions — as items of human experience, as part of the universe of discourse, they are different. And that difference, in part, is due to the fact that we use two different phraseological units to speak about them. It is not the world outside which we talk about but an inner world, the "*world of human experience*, the world as it is perceived within us, the universe of discourse". Even a scientist does not refer to the world outside (for linguistic signs do not refer) when he writes scientific papers, but rather translates "indices from that world into his own system of signs" (1973e). Meanings do not refer to the outside world, but rather SIGNIFY as part of a semiotic system. (Referring can only be done by semiotic means — e.g., by pointing.) And, the 'world of human experience' is, at least in part, a product of language itself and other semiotic systems (i.e. culture) of which we are a part and for which language is a fundamental basis. So, again, the items of experience are just like speech sounds in the sense that they owe their existence to the presence of meaning in a linguistic system. If humans did not have language, then *per force* the world of human experience would be quite different (and so would humans, for Jakobson quotes with approval Monod, who stated that "it is language which created humans, rather than humans language" — 1973e, 57). This is not to say that we may not have concepts or categories which are not directly based on linguistic concepts or categories — but all features of human experience are based ultimately on the fact that we all possess and use language. And certainly, the universe to which we refer is a semiotic one based on a system of signs:

Il est certes possible de renvoyer par le langage à quelque chose qui est (de fait) extra-linguistique. Il est cependant totalement exclu de se référer par lui à quelque chose d'absolument extra-sémiotique, quelque chose qui n'est pas à son tour déjà délimité sous forme de signes. Ce n'est pas l'univers du langage qui est clos mais l'univers des signes. L'opposition naïve entre langage et monde (extra-linguistique) doit être remplacée par une description plus complexe. (Holenstein, 1974, 186–7).

Furthermore, such concepts or categories of human experience which are linguistic in origin may, at the same time, be pure linguistic fictions having no support at all in ontological reality. The possibility of saying 'the sun rises' is important; we can talk about God and it is not important (linguistically) whether He exists or not. Moreover, it is extremely important how things are expressed (for every language can express every human thought or experience in more or less felicitous ways) — how the verbal means at our disposal organize what we say. The possibility of the formulation 'pursuit of happiness' is important for an understanding of the English language as a whole. From this point of view even rhetoric is part of linguistics, for it relies in good measure on the possibilities and impossibilities of a given language and on the definition of 'elegance' from the point of view of given systems. And of course, discourse, including poetic discourse, is a legitimate subject of inquiry for linguistic science.

Generic Nature of Sound and Meaning

One extremely important concomitant of the linguistic character of speech sounds and of meaning is the fact that both are always GENERIC in nature, whereas further specification comes from the surrounding (verbalized or verbalizable) context. Thus, the phoneme /p/ actually occurs in quite a variety of 'p' sounds, and the generic character of the /p/ as against the more specific character of the diverse contextual variants of the /p/ are provided for by the linguistic code. In like fashion, all words have, from the linguistic point of view, A GENERAL MEANING (a *Gesamtbedeutung*) in the sense that they correspond to general categories of human experience; again further specification comes from the context:

> Any symbol is endowed with general meaning, and the general meaning of any symbol, and of any verbal symbol in particular, has a generic character. Any further segmentation and individuation of the symbol is determined by its context. (1959c, 268)

This should be obvious in the case of *tree*, *go*, *when* — all of which have multiple contextual interpretations. This is also seen most clearly in the figurative uses of words. And the presence of the generic meaning of a word and thus of productive CONTEXTUAL INTERPRETATIONS shows the life of the generic character of meaning. Of course, the more highly marked a sign is, the more restricted its general meaning — but even words like *soufflé*, *demonstrate*, *collie*, etc. have multiple interpretations. PROPER NAMES also have multiple interpretations, in the sense that they potentially can be used for more than one person, place, or thing. This is the case even, for example, when the referent is more precise. Thus, the word *Napoleon* has a single, general meaning, while "the context indicates whether we speak of Napoleon in his infancy, at Austerlitz, in Moscow, in captivity, on his deathbed, or in posthumous legends, whereas his name in its general meaning encompasses all those stages of his life-span" (1959c, 268). If the word *Napoleon* is used, then it potentially can refer to all various views of Napoleon (the general meaning) as well as to any specific view. Similarly, SHIFTERS are also generic and have at the same time a general and a unitary meaning. *You*, from the point of view of the code, refers to the potential addressee of any potential utterance and introduces the necessity of the message to which it belongs as part of the meaning (1957a). The specific contextual application is known only when *you* is used in a given speech situation, in a given message. *My father* is a phrase consisting of a shifter (*my*) and a non-shifter (*father*), both of which have a generic meaning; in specific speech situations it may obtain a unique referent, although not necessarily in polyandrous societies or in a mythological context. Thus, all words have a general meaning inherent to their nature; more specific interpretations of that general meaning come from the use of the word in a given CONTEXT, both linguistic and extralinguistic.

Furthermore, even when signs are combined to form phrases, sentences, discourses, their reference is not unitary but still general (although less general than when used alone). If we take as simple a sentence as *he is at the house*, it is clear that the narrated event (1957a) is still different from and vaguer than any of the possible situations to which it refers. In particular, given the general meaning of *at*, the relationship between *he* and *the house* is not completely specified. We do not know if *he* is inside or outside, and if in either place exactly where *he* is located and what *he* is doing. Thus, the cues given by the speaker to the addressee in uttering this sentence for the specification of the possible referents of the utterance are general, vague, incomplete ones.

SELECTION/COMBINATION (SIMILARITY/CONTIGUITY)

Before delving more deeply into the relationship between form and meaning, we must first (briefly) explore a cardinal dichotomy in language (which cuts across the form/meaning distinction and yet at the same time provides much of the structuring of these two domains) between COMBINATION (the syntagmatic axis — where the combination may be either CONCURRENT or SEQUENTIAL) and SELECTION (the paradigmatic axis). As we shall see later, concurrent combination is one of the building blocks of linguistic structure. It is most evident in the case of the phoneme — a bundle (i.e. a concurrent combination) of distinctive features. Combinations are also evident with respect to morphemes and words. Latin *-mur* is, at the same time, passive (vs. the active *-mus*), first person (vs. the 2nd person *-mini*), plural (vs. the singular *-or*), and is, in Bally's terminology (1965), a "cumul des signifiés". Furthermore, syncretisms and homonymous forms can be looked on as concurrent combinations of several different meanings.

The relation between selection and combination points up certain principles of language patterning (e.g., its context-sensitivity, the relation between encoder and decoder, the opposition between general and contextual meaning) which will be discussed in more detail later in conjunction with the dichotomy of the signans and the signatum. In the case of selection, "a selection among alternatives implies the possibility of substituting one for the other, equivalent to the former in one respect and different from it in another. Actually, selection and substitution are two facets of the same operation." (1956b, 243) Selection is an internal relationship based on the SIMILARITY of the SUBSTITUTION SETS (including paradigms) which similarity ranges from the near identity of synonyms to the close relationship of antonyms, from resemblance (including homeoteleuton) to analogy, from metalanguage to metaphoric uses of terms, from more specification to less specification, from equivalence to contrast, from synonyms to heteronyms (and the whole problem of translation in general), from paraphrase to circumlocution. Moreover, on the time axis, substitution involves language change. Combination on the other hand is based on the external relation of CONTIGUITY, the concomitant combination of a given unit either concurrently with or in concatenation with other units. (Concatenation is of course the basis for Saussure's syntagmatic axis; 'bundling' was given no status in Saussure's two axes.) Moreover, any combination implies or creates a CONTEXT, thus pointing up the eminently CONTEXT-SENSITIVE nature of language:

> any sign is made up of constituent signs and/or occurs only in combination with other signs. This means that any linguistic unit at one and the same time serves as a context for simpler units and/or finds its own context in a more complex linguistic unit. Hence any actual grouping of linguistic units binds them into a superior unit: combination and contexture are two facets of the same operation. (1956b, 243)

Thus, combination involves the relationship of "neighborhood, proximity and remoteness, subordination and coordination" (1966f, 308) and, in addition, derivation and inflection. Moreover, relations of contiguity are the fundamental basis of predications. The opposition of selection and combination is the basis for many different and diverse dichotomies in language use, including METAPHOR (relationship by similarity) and METONYMY (relationship by contiguity), as well as the difference between lyric poetry (largely metaphorical) and epic poetry (largely metonymical). In addition:

> The poetic function projects the principle of equivalence from the axis of selection into the axis of combination. Equivalence is promoted to the constitutive device of the sequence. In poetry one syllable is equalized with any other syllable of the same sequence; word stress is assumed to equal word stress, as unstress equals unstress; prosodic long is matched with long, and short with short; word boundary equals word boundary, no boundary equals no boundary; syntactic pause equals syntactic pause, no pause equals no pause. Syllables are converted into units of measure, and so are morae or stresses. (1960a, 358)

Furthermore, surrealism, romanticism, and symbolism are all chiefly based (in different ways) on relations of similarity while realism and cubism are based (again in different ways) on relations of contiguity. Moreover, as Jakobson has shown in various papers, certain aphasic disorders may be roughly divided into SIMILARITY DISORDERS (sensory and afferent aphasia) as against CONTIGUITY DISORDERS (efferent aphasia), at least as two polar types. In the differentiation of encoder and decoder, for the encoder, selection is the antecedent (analytic) operation, while contexture is the subsequent (synthetic) operation, whereas the decoder is confronted with the synthesis and proceeds to the analysis. In ENCODING APHASIA, thus, the axis of combination is deficient, whereas in DECODING APHASIA the axis of selection is deficient. The external relation of contiguity applies also on the one hand to the temporal and spatial relation between speaker and addressee and on the other hand to the linkage between the components of the message and the context of which they are a part, while the internal relation of similarity applies to the equivalence of symbols between speaker and addressee on the one hand (thus restricting the notion of idiolect) and on the other hand to the linkage of the components of the message to the code.

The opposition between selection and combination is also at the basis of the opposition between the general (non-contextually determined) meaning of a given sign, which is revealed by the substitution of other signs, and its contextual meaning, which is determined by its connection with other signs within the same sequence. Moreover, iconic symbols are based on (a factual and conventional) similarity between form and meaning whereas indexical symbols are based on (a factual and conventional) contiguity between form and meaning. (Iconic symbols and indexical symbols are discussed and exemplified elsewhere.) Furthermore, in the realm of grammar, agreement is built on a relation of similarity whereas government is built on a relation of contiguity. And indeed, if we go to the realm of given messages:

> The addressee perceives that the given utterance (message) is a *combination* of constituent parts (sentences, words, phonemes, etc.) *selected* from the repository of all possible constituent parts (code). The constituents of a context are in a status of *contiguity* while in a substitution set signs are linked by various degrees of *similarity* which fluctuate between the equivalence of synonyms and the common core (*tertium comparationis*) of antonyms. (1957e, 159).

And, in fact, "syntax is concerned with the axis of concatenation, semantics with the axis of substitutions. ... Concatenation implies substitution." (1953c, 565) Thus the primacy of the units themselves is asserted; furthermore, we see that there is a marked/unmarked relationship between selection and combination, where selection is the unmarked category. Moreover, there is a further inequality between selection and combination because "selection deals with entities conjoined in the code" (1957e, 159) only. Combination deals with entities which are conjoined in the code and in the message simultaneously (particularly in the case of concurrent combinations — i.e., bundles of distinctive features — or in the case of concatenations such as the various combinations of phonemes making up words — both of these are combinations in both the code and the message) or only in the message (particularly in the case of phrases, clauses, sentences, discourses, the majority of which do not exist as fully codified combinations but as the less specified matrices).

But the boundary between selection and combination is a relative one, not an absolute one. In particular, equational predications ('a bachelor is an unmarried man') involve a "projection of a substitution set from the lexical code into the context of the given language" (1957e, 162). And concatenated units may, in terms of larger wholes, be seen as simultaneous — e.g., the concatenation of phonemes to form words. Furthermore, the possibilities of substitution for or selection of a word are defined by the concurrent elements (lexical and grammatical features) defining that word. If we look at the features themselves, paradigmatically they form a selection set, but in terms of phonemes, morphemes, words, etc. their simultaneous combination is uppermost. With respect to the context-sensitive nature of language, possibilities of selection are governed both by the presence in the linguistic system of the other paradigmatic choices available and by the presence in the context of other choices made. Furthermore, as we shall see, the hierarchy of linguistic elements is determined by the paradigmatic set of which that element is a part, by the way in which the elements combine concurrently, and by the sequential constraints on the given element. Finally, in phonology, the inherent features are defined in terms of the presence vs. absence of a given acoustic trait in a given place and do not need the sequence for their comparison and recognition: the invariant of /k/ is defined independently of the context and /k/ can be recognized independently of the context. On the other hand, the prosodic features depend on their use in a sequence where the polar opposites both occur: a long vowel is 'longer than' in a given sequence.

PART II

SPECIFICS OF STRUCTURE

Language, then, is a relatively autonomous, self-contained, goal-directed, dynamic, creative, semiotic entity in which there is dialectic tension between selection on the one hand and combination on the other. In a sense, the core of the structure of language for Jakobson is made up of three interrelated and interdependent notions:

(1) The LINGUISTIC SIGN as the indissoluble connection of SIGNANS and SIGNATUM and (a) the close relationship between SIGNANS and SIGNATUM, (b) the GENERIC character of both the SIGNANS and the SIGNATUM, (c) the SIGNANS as a structuring imposed on speech sounds and the SIGNATUM as a structuring imposed on the world of human experience.

(2) the importance of RELATIONS for defining the units of language (rather than vice versa) and particularly the eminent importance of the concept of OPPOSITION as a mutually implicating and dependent relation between two terms which reciprocally 'call for' and 'educe' each other — neither can exist without the other. Thus the concept of opposition necessarily entails BINARISM for Jakobson (cf. Pos) — 'opposites', logically speaking, come in two's. Furthermore, these opposites are always in some sort of MARKED/UNMARKED relationship, where the marked term gives more information than the unmarked term of the given opposition. MARKEDNESS is part of the characterization of opposition.

(3) The notion of RELATIONAL INVARIANCE and its opposition with CONTEXTUAL VARIATION. This entails a bifurcation of the more general signans from its more specific, contextually determined implementations and of the more general signatum from its more specific, contextually determined interpretations. All of these are mutually dependent: the notion of opposition rests on relational invariance and in addition is the major means by which language 'creates' sound and/or items of human experience. The linguistic sign is based on the opposition of signans/signatum, both of which are relationally invariant and related,

most importantly, by opposition (i.e. by markedness) to the rest of the linguistic signs in the given system. Since I must discuss these notions in some linear order, I will do first the nature of the linguistic sign, then the notion of relations and in particular the general concept of opposition, then relational invariance, before finally discussing markedness.

LINGUISTIC SIGN

If we look at language in terms of its use, we see that it is primarily a way of employing sound[1] to convey information, i.e., sounds are related to information through language, which creates semiotic data both out of sound and out of the world of human experience by integrating them. The most important integrating factor for the signans and the signatum is the LINGUISTIC SIGN (*signum*), a necessary, dependent, and indissoluble duality, a combination of a *signans* (or, in the English translation of Saussure's *signifiant*: 'signifier') and of a *signatum* ('signified', for *signifié*) where neither part of the duality can exist nor be understood except in terms of its function within the sign. Although this view of the linguistic sign is similar to that of Saussure, it will be clear as we proceed that Jakobson operates with purely semiotic data and is in this respect closer to classical theories of the sign (see 1959a; 1959c; 1973e; 1975b). He objects not only to the psychologistic and vague Saussurian terms *image acoustique* and *concept*, but also to the Saussurian view of the sign as:

because the word *arbre* (whether in its graphic or phonetic rendering) and the drawing are not parts of a sign but signs in themselves (1959c). Each has a signans (in the case of *arbre* its phonetic or graphic shape and in the case of its pictorial representation) and each has a signatum (the meaning assigned to the concept 'tree' in French). Moreover, the rela-

[1]Of course, it can also be done without sounds, but sound is the primary means.

tion between 🌳 and its signatum is iconic. Since both 🌳 and *arbre* have a similar signatum, this is a case of intersemiotic translation or transmutation (1959a).

We have already noted a very close parallel between the signans and the signatum in the sense that each is a classification creating linguistically based units: in the case of the signans, speech sounds, and in the case of the signatum, items of human experience. Furthermore, both the signans and the signatum are GENERIC in nature and subject to (contextual) individuation and specification. However, there is an essential difference between the signans and the signatum in the sense that the signans is itself PERCEIVABLE directly (it literally occurs in the sound matter): human beings utter speech sounds and the phonemes in a given language literally 'occur' in the sounds. But the signatum is INTELLIGIBLE (or 'TRANSLATABLE' or 'CONCEPTUAL'). It is carried by the signans only because of their mutual dependency in the linguistic sign. Signata are not 'uttered' nor do we 'carry' signata around on our backs (1953c, 567). The signata are 'carried' by the signantia only by virtue of the fact that they co-exist in the linguistic sign. And in fact, the signantia exist for the express purpose of carrying signata — the material is given only as a means of transferring something else (the meaning). The linguistic sign, then, is not only an example of a means (signans)/ends (signatum) relationship but also of a TRANSFER — of matter which is given only as a transfer to the meaning, of matter which transfers something in addition to itself.

Moreover, as we have seen, the signatum is essentially different from the supposedly ontological reality; the world of human experience is rather created by or dependent upon the existence of language than vice versa. Signata, then, are not open to direct observation nor are they apprehendable by other than semiotic means. Jakobson, following Peirce, has expressed the fact that the signatum of a given word can only be made intelligible to one unfamiliar with that word through translation either within the same language (intralingual translation or rewording, synonyms, paraphrases, etc.) or between languages (interlingual translation or translation proper) (1959a). Linguistic units are understandable generally only through the use of other linguistic units. It may of course be possible also to use non-linguistic but semiotic means (intersemiotic translation or transmutation). We have already seen an example of this in the transmutational relationship between 🌳 and *arbre* in French. However, intersemiotic translation may be dangerous if the semiotic signs have different statuses in different cultures. Pointing, for instance, can be a malediction in one culture and a means of identification in another. Moreover, as he himself has said:

> Suppose I want to explain to a unilingual Indian what Chesterfield is, and I point to a package of cigarettes. What can the Indian conclude? He doesn't know whether I mean this package in particular, or a package in general, one cigarette or many, a certain brand or cigarettes in general, or, still more generally, something to smoke, or, universally, any agreeable thing. He doesn't know, moreover, whether I'm simply showing, giving, selling, or prohibiting the cigarettes to him. He will gather what Chesterfield is, and what it is not, only if he masters a series of other linguistic signs which will serve as interpretant of the sign under discussion. (1953c, 566–7)

This means basically that the system of signata is a closed one and cannot be fully understood except through linguistic means — but even this is imperfect, since no synonyms or paraphrases are exact equivalents of the original unit, nor is intralingual translation ever completely satisfactory. This means that signata are understandable only in and of themselves — in their relationship to the signans in the linguistic sign and in terms of their systematic structure.

From Signatum to Signans

It is extremely important as I pointed out above to realize that although both the signans and signatum are CODE-GIVEN TRUTHS, only the former actually occur in and thus are perceivable in speech sounds. This means that languages have no other way of conveying SIGNATA than by their SIGNANTIA either on a sound level or by a substitutional written form.

This has several consequences for the nature of language. First of all, since, according to Jakobson, language has no other way of conveying meaning than through the formal properties of linguistic signs, meanings are always a fortiori connected with some form in the language. "There is no signatum without a signum" (1959a, 260) (and, *a fortiori*, without a signans). Of course, certain signata may be correlated with a ZERO SIGNANS, but this zero is recognized as such through its opposition to overt formal expressions (e.g., the singular is recognized as such in English even though it has no overt formal representation because of its opposition to the overt formally expressed plural). If concepts like 'agent', 'animateness', 'passive voice', etc. exist in a given language, then their existence is due to their correlation with a given form or with a given FORMAL OPPOSITION in that language. As a further consequence, if, for example, a case system exists in a language, it is because case has a function to fulfill with respect to communicating information and that function is different from, e.g., the prepositional system, word order, etc. Furthermore, the fact that what is conveyed by a case system in one language may be conveyed in certain instances by prepositions in another is of course typologically extremely interesting, but it does not establish the synonymy of cases or interchangeability of cases and prepositions as general categories, for each includes certain uses and certain types of information which the other does not have. Each must be studied in and of itself. At the same time, it should be understood that the non-existence of a given category in a language is also significant. To impute 'case' on some 'deep' level to a language which has no morphologically expressed case system is to confuse the formal means of structuring the semantic system with the kinds of information which any language must, ultimately, in some way, express. On the other hand, the formal means of expressing a particular system are themselves relevant because they show differences in types of classification. Thus, English has a gender system (expressed through the pronominal differences *he*, *she*, *it* and *who*, *which*, *what*) — so, to say that there is no classification would be wrong. On the other hand, gender in English and gender in French are quite different, not only in the degree of formal expression but also in the distribution of their semantic values.

Furthermore, different meanings are generally connected with different forms because differences in meaning can only be inherently communicated by differences in form. Cases of HOMONYMY do not invalidate the sign relationship. In fact, as Karcevskij (1929) has shown, they may be necessary for the sign relationship. In any case, they underline the difference between signans and signatum. Furthermore, homonymous signs may be linguistically disambiguated when used in larger syntactic matrices or when embedded in a larger discourse: in fact, they require, for their discernment, a differentiating context.

From Signans to Signatum

Moreover, there is no signans without a signatum (or *a fortiori* without a signum): each form is connected to a meaning. Jakobson has pointed out (1939b; 1940) that an overt form may actually correspond to a lack of meaning ('zero meaning'), i.e., to the UNMARKED MEANING in a marked/unmarked opposition. This is the case for example with the 3rd person singular of the present tense of the verb in English: the overt *-s* corresponds to 3 unmarked categories (3rd person, singular, present tense).

Other cases of a zero signatum for an overt signans (1957e; 1959c) may include the use by a speaker of a new or unfamiliar word which conforms to the phonological structure of the language but for which the addressee has no meaning. It is of course significant that he expects there to be a signatum ('there is no signans without a signatum') and that he assumes that this signatum is different from that of all other words in the language ('for every differnce in form there is a concomitant and associated difference in meaning'). So the presence of both a 'zero signans' and a 'zero signatum' is carefully based on the relations between the units and the possibilities of commutation and substitution.

The fact that there is no signans without a signatum means, in particular, that the phonological distinctive features, the phoneme itself, as well as such normally considered meaningful units as the word, are signs and that furthermore, they have a signatum, which accounts for their status as a sign. The search for the signatum has led to the division between 'PHONOLOGY' and 'GRAMMAR' not in the sense that the first is uniquely the domain of form while the second is uniquely the domain of meaning — for both are both formal and meaningful (i.e. sign systems) — but rather in the type of information conveyed. And in any case, there is no absolute boundary between the two — they are only relatively autonomous. This is evidenced, for example, in the use of the phoneme /m/ in case inflections marked with [+ marginality] in Russian. (See my discussion later on the relation between phonology and grammar.)

I will be using the term 'phonology' for that part of linguistics concerned with units which are signans-based or signans-oriented and which moreover function within meaningful units. That part of linguistics which is concerned with constituents having their own meaning — i.e. those units which are signatum-based or signatum-oriented (i.e. the domain of true signification) is usually divided up by Jakobson into GRAMMAR (morphology and syntax) and LEXICOLOGY (vocabulary or lexicon and phraseology). No general cover term exists in Jakobson's writings for this domain,[2] but since Jakobson's own explorations in this area

[2] Jakobson objects to the term 'semantics' as a general cover term on the grounds that (1) it may not include grammar and thus will imply too narrow an interpretation; in fact for Jakobson grammar is more 'semantic' than anything else because grammar is obligatory in the sense that a choice between alternatives is forced upon the speaker; (2) it may include phonology and thus imply too wide an interpretation; (3) it may include only grammatical concepts and not grammatical processes (formal aspects of the meaning constituents) and thus is too narrow.

are in the domain of grammar (obligatory and oppositional in nature), I will often speak of grammar and grammatical features; when speaking of vocabulary (an area Jakobson often mentions and opposes to grammar as being non-obligatory and not based on a consistent system of oppositions, especially in the nominal system, but in which he has done little work thus far), I will speak of the LEXICON and 'lexical features'. To correspond to the overall domain of signification or conceptual meaning, I will use (at Jakobson's suggestion) the term 'CONCEPTUAL FEATURES'. (Jakobson has said that he was inspired by Sapir's (1921) use of 'concept'.) In any case, the term 'DISTINCTIVE' feature is reserved solely for phonology, as 'distinctive' here refers to the type of signatum tied with the features and phonemes — it carries only the notion of otherness — while 'conceptual' will apply to the significative signatum.

To get back to the fact that there is no signans without a signatum and to the consequences this has for the different types of signata tied to signantia, the phoneme is by this definition an informational unit: its meaning is 'MERE OTHERNESS' — that is, the signatum is purely distinctive, for phonemes serve only to differentiate formally between given units. They do not have intrinsically any other signata, although problems of synesthesia as well as of the interrelation of phonology and semantics show that further functions may be added to this distinctive one. But in the hierarchy of functions, the distinctive one is uppermost. Furthermore, the features may have, besides the distinction of words of different meanings, configurative, expressive or redundant functions.[3] On the other hand, the meaning of a morpheme or a word is conceptual — in addition to being different from the meaning of all the other units at their level, they intrinsically convey some information about the world of human experience. Thus, the accusative case in Russian inherently gives a 'reference point' for the verbal process; and in the two large classes of syntactically different uses of this same case, the reference point may have a contextual meaning either in terms of its goal or in terms of a temporal overlap.

Thus, no form exists without some meaningful function to fulfill, and *a fortiori* formal differences are always meaningful (communicative). It is on this basis that the difference between strong and weak verbs in English, between *en* and *dans* in French (Waugh 1976b), etc. are assumed to be meaningful. On the one hand, synonymy in the sense of a full equi-

[3]And of course, other elements besides the distinctive features can function as redundant, configurative, and expressive features.

valence in meaning, equivalence in the categorization found in the code, does not exist: in some respect the two 'synonymous' signs are different. Nor on the other hand do non-functional (i.e. arbitrary) formal differences exist. The possibility of setting up distributional rules which might account for certain of the differences (e.g., for *en* vs. *dans*, *dans* is more often used before a determiner than *en* is — Waugh 1976) does not invalidate the meaning difference: first of all, the complementary distribution is almost never complete; and second of all, even in those cases where there is no possibility of substitution, the inherent meaning of the given sign used is still valid. Thus, for instance, as Jakobson has often stated (see in particular 1958b), if *k* is always followed by the dative in Russian then this invalidates neither the meaning of *k* nor the meaning of the dative, for the meaning of *k* is based on its presence in the substitution set *k*, *na*, *po*, *za*, etc., and of the larger substitution sets *k* + dative vs. *po* + dative, etc. The meaning of the dative is based on its place in the paradigmatic set exemplified by the case system (nominative/accusative/dative/instrumental etc.). Meanings are established by paradigmatic relations. The meaning is not cancelled because of the lack of substitution in a given context (i.e. because the dative case can be replaced by no other case after *k*). Furthermore, there is no parallel predictiveness here: the *k* may predict the dative, but the dative does not predict *k*, thus showing the relative autonomy of the two. But this point is extremely important — in this sense the distinctive features and grammatical features are essentially different: the distinctive features are merely distinctive ('mere otherness') so a lack of commutation in a given context robs them of their distinctive nature in that context. Thus, in phonology, we can and we should speak about NEUTRALIZATION, or better 'DEFECTIVE PHONEMES' (1978). Since the information carried by a phoneme is 'mere otherness', in those cases where commutation cannot occur, the opposition between phonemes in terms of their meaning is not relevant nor is the opposition between those features which do not function in a certain context. But in semantics, if commutation is not possible, a morpheme, or a word, can not lose its meaning because the meaning is more than 'mere otherness': the grammatical features for example give some kind of positive information. Lack of commutation in a given context does not rob them of their information. It remains and in fact it may explain why commutation is not possible: it is the meaning of a given sign which does not allow for its use in given contexts. The distribution of a sign then, may be studied, but it must be remembered that distribution is a formal and a semantic phenomenon and that distribution is but a means to an end.

Furthermore, within the linguistic system itself, there may be 'holes', combinations of conceptual features which are logically possible but not provided with a form. There may be other signs which stand in a marked relationship to the 'hole', thus creating an imbalance, but this IMBALANCE does not rob the more marked signs of their meaning. The fact that 'deponent' verbs in Latin are not supplied with an active counterpart does not mean that the 'deponents' are expressly less passive than those verbs which have a full (formal) active/passive opposition. The passive morpheme, in this case, cannot be considered as non-significant. Thus, the indiscriminate application of all criteria from phonology to semantics leads to errors in analysis and is due to not recognizing the relative autonomy of each of the domains and the *differentia specifica* of each — the kind of meaning associated with the linguistic sign in each.

REDUNDANCY in both phonology and on the higher levels of language is relevant in that redundant items inform about the concurrent context (only in phonology) and/or sequential context (in all domains) (1971i, 20). But, again in phonology, the redundant (and configurative) features have a single specific signification (1971i, 20) while the distinctive features have only 'mere otherness'. On the other hand, the redundancy may, particularly in elliptical speech, whispering, emphatic speech, under conditions of noise, etc., take over the distinctive function (see 1968a; 1971i). In grammar, etc., redundancy also plays a role, but it must be emphasized again that redundant items not only may refer to the concurrent or sequential context but they have in addition their full conceptual function. Thus, for instance, agreement of the adjective with the noun in French shows the relation of the adjective to the noun (and may disambiguate as to which noun is actually being modified), and informs about the gender of the noun and thus may disambiguate between homonymous nouns with different genders. In any case, the gender of the adjective (even when completely predictable and non-disambiguating) carries the full significance of gender itself.

A further concomitant of the relation between form and meaning is that formal differences exist because they have a communicative function to fulfill: 'for every difference in form there is a concomitant and associated difference in meaning'. And conversely, because of the close tie between form and meaning, it is assumed that wherever there is a sameness of form (i.e., where the only formal differences which may exist are due to the relatively autonomous internal workings of the phonological system of the language), there is to be expected (aside from cases of homonymy[4]) a sameness of meaning. This so-called ONE FORM-ONE MEANING[5] principle is extremely important, methodologically: if the linguist does not look for sameness of meaning, he will never find it. The concepts 'sameness of form', 'sameness of meaning' bring up another point — (RELATIONAL) INVARIANCE—which defines the nature of the linguistic sign and thus is inherent to this discussion. I will not, however, discuss relational invariance here, but will leave that for later, as it has far-reaching ramifications and deserves special attention.

No Compulsory Arbitrariness

An extremely important part of Jakobson's view of the linguistic sign, which differentiates his thought from that of Saussure and many other linguists, is the NON-NECESSARY ARBITRARINESS of the linguistic sign, in terms of the relation between the signans and the signatum. It is of course evident that from an external point of view, the relationship between the signans and the signatum is in most cases arbitrary and the sign is in this case (in Peirce's terminology) a pure symbol. Non-arbitrariness from the external point of view does occur, particularly in the case of synesthesia. If we take an internal point of view, the picture is much more complicated. Saussure himself mentioned examples of secondary motivation (e.g., in derived words and compounds, and grammatical paradigms); onomatopoeia bridges the gap between the external and the internal; and phonesthemes (e.g., Engl. *gl-*, *sl-*, *fl-*, *-ash* — Bolinger, 1950) show a partial motivation. Moreover, Jakobson has always insisted upon the fact that, from an internal linguistic point

[4]In Russian, there are case syncretisms in various declensions where e.g. the nominative and accusative fall together. Yet the accusative exists in Russian through the formal differences expressed not by all words but by certain words. In such instances, we are allowed to speak of homonyms — i.e., the recognition of homonymy depends on the existence of formal differences elsewhere in the system and the associated semantic value of those differences. On the other hand, in the English pronominal system, the accusative and dative are not differentiated formally (both being rendered by the pronouns *me*, *him*, *her*, *us*, *them*). This accounts, says Jakobson, for the presence of the two passives in English: *he was given the book*, *the book was given to him*. The accusative and dative are not differentiated and thus may pattern similarly.

[5]The formulation 'one form — one meaning' is one used informally by van Schooneveld in discussing Jakobson's work. It does not appear in Jakobson's own writings.

of view, even in the symbol the connection between form and meaning is not arbitrary from the point of view of the linguistic system itself — the connection between them is a necessary, even if CONVENTIONALIZED, one. But perhaps the major insight into the non-arbitrariness of the linguistic sign comes from Peirce's differentiation between ICON, INDEX and SYMBOL (see 1966a) and Jakobson has pointed out that it is only in the latter (an imputed contiguity between signans and signatum) that the relationship between form and meaning can be said to be truly arbitrary, from an extra-linguistic point of view.

ICONICITY — a factual similarity between signans and signatum — is extremely pervasive in language and with regard to the most diverse phenomena (see 1966a). Thus, for instance, the order of elements may reflect priority in time ('*veni, vidi, vici*') or in logical terms ('the President and the Secretary of State') or in syntactic terms (the precedence of the subject over the object in the unmarked word order in nearly all the languages of the world). Furthermore, in various Indo-European languages, the positive, comparative, and superlative degrees of adjectives show a "gradual increase in the number of phonemes, e.g. *high — higher — highest, altus, altior, altissimus*" (1966a, 352). And in all languages where a plural exists distinct from the singular, no language would normally designate the singular by an additional morpheme while the plural would be devoid of such a morpheme. In his study of the relationship between Russian stem suffixes and verbal aspects, Jakobson has noted an ICONIC CONGRUENCE between the meanings of the two aspects and their correlated forms. Specifically, "the perfective signalizes a limited extent of the narrated event, and correspondingly a lesser number of phonemes characterizes the perfective stem suffix. . . . The same semantic relation between the two aspects is reflected by the phonemic opposition diffuse vs. compact or non-compact vs. compact. . . . since the scale of magnitude, i.e., the small vs. large symbolism is 'latently connected for the average listener with the opposition of diffuse and compact' (1952, 2.413)" (1966g, 199). In his study of the Ukranian imperative Jakobson has shown that, morphologically, the imperative is most usually 'an approximation to the bare verb stem' and phonologically is 'treated as a type of particle' (1965b). This special form of the imperative — distinguishing it from the declarative — parallels its special meaning, which tends to shun truth values and to exhibit conative rather than referential features.

Furthermore, in the relation between signans and grammatical signatum, there is a specialization of certain phonemes or combinations of phonemes (e.g., the alveolars in English grammatical suffixes, the phoneme *-m* in Russian for the marginal cases, etc.). Moreover, partial similarity in the signans can produce an effect of synchronic connection even there where none exists etymologically (e.g., French *ami-ennemi*; Eng. *father, mother, brother*; Eng. *two, twelve, twice, twenty, twin*; English *-ash* in *bash, mash, crash, clash*, etc. — see 1966a). Such examples (and others discussed in particular in 1966a) show that iconicity is prevalent in language and deserves much more attention than it has hitherto been given.

The second type of non-arbitrariness is that of INDEXICAL SYMBOLS (or SHIFTERS) since they show a (factual) contiguity between signans and signatum, especially as they point to the speech event in which they are used for their interpretation. We have already discussed indexical symbols above on page 24.

Intimate Connection of Signans and Signatum

Another extremely important conclusion from this view that the relationship between the signans and the signatum is an intimate one and that meanings are necessarily and essentially tied to forms is that it is not at all the case, according to Jakobson, that the 'surface' or formal properties of any linguistic unit whatsoever do not provide sufficient information for the communication of meaning. (The relationship between form and meaning is, from this point of view, not arbitrary.) They do provide sufficient information — and in fact they must — for the only information a hearer gets via the speech signal are the sounds themselves. Thus, whatever is semantically relevant for the hearer must be carried by the speech signal — the forms are directly connected with a meaning and both are communicated by the speech signal. (This means in particular that ambiguity and homonymy may provide problems in interpretation for the hearer, while the speaker may either be unaware of the plight of the hearer or may deliberately use the confusion for obscuring his intended meaning or may 'play' with the different possibilities (as in puns).) Of course, possibilities of ambiguity are always avoidable through further clarification by the context.

COMPLEXES of meaning are conveyed by complexes of forms arranged into phrases, clauses, sentences, discourses, etc. — the foundation of which are the matrices which give such fundamental syntagmatic relationships as attribution, predication, verb + object, preposition +

object, etc. The sentence is a whole composed of smaller parts, and no understanding of the whole can be gained without a prior understanding of the parts, nor is the whole completely different from or separate from the parts.

But an extremely important question which can be posed with regard to units like the phoneme, the word, the sentence, etc. is which units exist as such in the linguistic system and which do not. (The question is not which have meaning and which do not, for they all have meaning.) Jakobson's answer has been unequivocal — the word is the largest unit which is codified as such. He assumes under the rubric 'word' also compounds, e.g. *floodlight*, word phrases, which by convention are codified as such, e.g. *church key* (in the sense of bottle opener), *how are you*, proverbs (see 1966c, 637 ff.), etc. Certain phraseological expressions or conventional phrases like *nice girl* are on the border between words and freely coined expressions; one can, however, discern the meaning of the whole from the meaning of the parts. Normally, above the word level, one encounters what Jakobson has called 'syntactic matrices', prefabricated, codified molds or cadres, for which are chosen for use in given messages particular lexical items. Such matrices include subject-predicate, preposition-object, adjective-noun, verb-object, and so forth. The matrices may be looked upon as a type of pattern which may be extended analogically to new expressions by the (relatively) free combination of lexical items. The matrix is provided for by the linguistic code, but given combinations, e.g. *green rug*, *magnificant girl*, *beautiful tree* are not.[6] The insertion of particular lexical items in such matrices is not, for the most part, dictated by linguistic rules. It is a great mistake to confuse linguistically impossible combinations and those which don't conform to an absolutist view of ontological reality (*pregnant man*, *golf plays John*, *colorless green ideas*, etc.). 'Syntactic meaning' and 'sentential meaning' are thus inherently different from (but related to) the meanings of the codified units. The meaning of a unit is part of the system proper; the meaning of a sentence is based on the syntactic matrices and combinatory, contextual possibilities. Furthermore, a language is not a set (finite or infinite) of ready-made sentences, but rather a system of signs and of matrices.

Another very important conclusion from the fact that the relationship between form and meaning is an intimate one is the nature of

[6]This is evident in child language acquisition, where children 'practice' various lexical combinations. See 1962d.

the relationship between the phonological and sematological (especially grammatical and lexical) aspects of language (1949e), part of which relationship is sometimes called MORPHONOLOGY or 'morphophonemics'. Some relevant questions about the nature of the relationship are: are there formal means which are peculiarly suited to specific kinds of meanings? Are there recognizable types of formal neutralizations that take place between signs in a given category and can these neutralizations be explained through the meanings expressed? Why is it that differences in grammatical meaning tend to be expressed by systematic differences in formal shape, while differences in lexical meaning tend to produce arbitrary differences in lexical shape? Why is it that certain semantic differences are expressed by iconic differences in shape while others are not? On what grounds does one recognize the 'base' form for the description of alternations and what relationship does this form have to the meanings of the alternants? What influence do sound changes have on the grammatical system? On the other hand, how are phonemic changes grammatically limited? What does all this tell us about the relation between form and meaning? In relation to this Jakobson has always contended that it is not justified to speak of so-called morphologically-conditioned (non-automatic) alternation as if the alternation had purely formal consequences and revealed no semantic differences. The morpheme is first and foremost a semantic unit, or at least a unit in which the semantic layer is just as important as the formal layer. A typical example of this is the 'strong verbs' in English; might it not be the case that they as a class (or a series of sub-classes) share some lexical feature or features, which account for their formal behavior? The feature may be difficult to find or define, but that does not invalidate its existence. Similarly, the division into declensions and conjugations, of Latin verbs and nouns, would be due not so much to meaning-less categories but rather to meaning-full[7] ones.

Other concrete examples of Jakobson's concern with the relation between the signans and the signatum come from, for example, his definition of CONFIGURATIVE (either CULMINATIVE or DEMARCATIVE) and EXPRESSIVE features:

[7] This is not to say that such meaning correlations will be easy to find but, just as it has been found for the semantic analysis of such categories as case that the meanings tend to be abstract, so it is likely that categories like declension, conjugation, 'strong verb', gender, etc. are also abstract.

CONFIGURATIVE FEATURES signal the division of the utterance into grammatical units of different degrees of complexity, particularly into sentences and words, either by singling out these units and indicating their hierarchy (CULMINATIVE FEATURES) or by delimiting and integrating them (DEMARCATIVE FEATURES). EXPRESSIVE FEATURES OF EMPHATICS put the relative emphasis on different parts of the utterance or on different utterances and suggest the emotional attitudes of the utterer. (1971i, 20)

Word stress in English is culminative (and distinctive) while word stress in Czech is demarcative; certain kinds of contrastive stress in English are expressive ('she is *so* nice'). In Russian, the less obscure variety of the phoneme /i/ in /ispompi líl/ '(one) poured from a pump', as against the more obscure variety of the phoneme /i/ in /ˈkrugóm pilíl/ '(one) spread dust all around', has a configurative function: "The less obscure variety appears only immediately before the stressed syllable of the same word and thus displays a configurative feature: it signals that no word boundary follows immediately." (1971i, 21) (Negative border marks — see also 1949e — can be just as important as positive ones.) Expressive features may be exemplified by the fact that /pilíl/ may be uttered "with a prolongation of the first, pretonic vowel [ɯ:] to magnify the narrated event, or with a prolongation of the second, accented vowel [:í] [sic] to imply a burst of emotion." (1971i, 21) Configurative and expressive features are essentially different from distinctive features in that they concern a differentiation of specific signata while the distinctive features only convey 'mere otherness'. Moreover, the configurative and expressive features are not necessarily binary while the distinctive features are.

Another example of the relationship between the phonemes of a given linguistic system and the grammatical system concerns PHONEME COMBINATIONS:

If our inquiry is concerned with the phonemes of a given language and we attempt to draw up the net of their actual combinations, we must inevitably take into account the grammatical entities: the combinations of phonemes are different at the beginning, within, and at the end of a word. The combinations at the juncture of two formal units — for instance, of a prefix or suffix and the adjacent parts of a word — differ from the internal combinations, and also the laws of clustering at prefix and suffix junctures can be dissimilar (for instance, Russian admits a hiatus only at the juncture of a radical with a prefix or with another radical — a word with a prefix is conceived as a kind of compound). Functionally different formal units are often denoted by different phonemic configurations (in Slavic languages, for instance, suffixes are clearly distinguished from radicals by their phonemic contours). The radicals of different parts of speech (for instance, of nouns and verbs, or of nouns and pronouns) can be differentiated by the length and composition of the phoneme sequence.

In Gilyak, phoneme combinations which are usual in propria, particularly in personal names, do not occur in common words. Thus an overall inventory of phoneme combinations is a fiction, because every class of grammatical units and every position within these units has its own roster of phonemic combinations. (1949e, 106–7)

In the discussion of iconicity above, we mentioned other examples of the relation between the signans and the signatum, in particular the specialization of certain phonemes for desinence as against stem and, within the desinences, for a particular subclass of desinences. As the concluding part ("The Grammatical Processes of the Russian Verb") of his masterful article "Shifters" (1957a) Jakobson deals with the order relation which the various grammatical categories have with the stem and with the various phonic means of rendering the categories. He concludes with the following statement:

the expression of the Russian verbal categories roughly exhibits the following pattern:

The P-designators (designators of the participants), whether shifters (person) or non-shifters (gender and number), make use of the final desinential suffixes.

The E-designators (designators of the event) deal with word-components anterior to the final suffix. The shifters (tense) employ initial desinential suffixes, while the non-shifters (aspect) go farther back; they ignore the desinence and operate with the stem — its suffixes and prefixation.

The connectors widely use units posterior to the final suffix. The non-shifters (voice and taxis) deal with the postfixes, while the shifters (mood) tend to reduce the desinence to zero and to replace the usual desinential suffixes by autonomous annexes, partly by changing the former into the latter, partly by adding new, purely modal particles (1957a, 146)

His two studies of the Russian case system (1936, 1958b) both contain a study of CASE SYNCRETISM and an analysis of these syncretisms from the point of view of which oppositions are likely to be cancelled, which are not, which may or may not be, and how all these collapses interact. There is an attempt to see the syncretisms in terms of the total system rather than as isolated occurrences. With respect to the interaction of case and number, he has also investigated the relationship between genitive and plural and in particular between nominative singular and genitive plural in terms of the formal opposition: zero desinence/actual desinence, whereas the distinction of nominative plural and genitive singular is generally given in terms of word stress placement (1957b). The relationship between the genitive and number is based on the fact that both are 'quantifiers'. And of course the question of zeros in both the signans and the signatum as well as the interaction of a zero in one with a non-zero in the other was the subject of his study 'Signe zéro' (1939b — discussed above). And, of course, iconic and indexical relations (discussed above) between the signans and the signatum reveal the intimate connection between the two.

STRUCTURE: RELATIONS

Language is not simply an agglomeration of linguistic signs — the signs themselves form a system, the defining characteristics of which are at the same time the defining characteristics of language in general. Language is 'systematic' in the sense that it is structured, in the sense that it is a complete, self-regulating entity. But STRUCTURE, like everything else we have seen, has a specific definition in Jakobson's view. In a sense structure implies, and is implied by, relative autonomy, teleology, efficiency, redundancy, creativity, the non-material nature of language, the dyad of code and message, the opposition of selection and combination, the bifurcation into signans and the more specific sounds and into signatum and the more specific contextual meanings. One could define the structure of language (paraphrasing Erlich 1955, 199, who in turn was rephrasing Tynjanov), as 'a complex whole, characterized by the interrelatedness and dynamic tension between individual components and held together by the underlying unity of the communicative function'. Furthermore, language is LAW-GOVERNED — there are strict laws of structural integration which mean not only that language is more than a mechanical aggregate of component parts but also that the types of integration are strictly governed. Some of the law-governed character of language has been discussed previously — and indeed a discussion of structure implies and is implied by a notion of LAWFUL INTEGRATION.

Language is a structured entity in which everything is, in some way and by some means, related to everything else, in a paradigmatic hierarchical structure. Language is a RELATIONAL ENTITY, a NETWORK OF RELATIONS. At any level of structure it is the relations which are the most important. Each item has a place in the overall pattern, especially with respect to the communicative function, and this place determines its inherent nature as well as its relationship to everything else. At the same time, its inherent nature and relationship to everything else determines its place in the pattern: there is an overall dependency of mutual implication. It is also Jakobson's contention that the items themselves exist only because of their relations to other items in the system: the items are set up by the relations themselves. The relations are primary. That which defines a given unit is at the same time that which relates it (through EQUIVALENCE and DIFFERENCE) to the other units in the system; or to put it more accurately, that which differentiates an item from the other items of the system is also that which defines it. Thus, given the relatively autonomous nature of the phoneme, the separation of the phoneme from its material support, the semiotic status of the phoneme including its status as a linguistic sign, its interrelations with all the other phonemes in the system, its dependence upon the system itself for its definition and for its inherent nature, then we see why Jakobson agrees with the pioneering Cubist painter Braque in stating: "I do not believe in things, I believe only in their relationship." (1962g, 632). Phonemes do not exist except as terms in relations; 'things' do not exist except in so far as they relate to other 'things' and to the system of which they are a part. This is an extremely difficult point and one which perhaps more than any other has been misunderstood. We are used to thinking in terms of things in and of themselves. But as Jakobson has pointed out (in personal communication) 'yellow' is nothing by itself — it is only by comparing it with 'green' or with 'black' and 'white' that we can understand its inherent nature. It is the relation of 'yellow' to the other colors which gives it its essence. So, from the methodological point of view, no item can be understood except by determining its place in the pattern — that is, by studying its internal nature with respect to all the other points in the structure, by determining its relation to the system.

This means first of all that an atomistic methodology will always fall short of discerning the structure of language, since atomism is not one of the defining characteristics of language. Secondly, it means that any analysis whatsoever must from the beginning lead us *in medias res* — everything is connected to everything else. Thirdly, it means that, in terms of language structure, the explanation for a particular phenomenon is given in terms of the place of that phenomenon in the system — in terms of the communicative function of language. Fourthly, it means that the over-all structure is unitary in terms of relations (i.e., there is no assumption of absolutely autonomous components, but at the same time no assumption of an undifferentiated monolith). Fifthly, it means that language is a paradigmatic structure of structures — a structure consisting of relationships between the constituent elements. Sixthly, it means that no part of language is, in Jakobson's view, unstructured (although some parts may be more or less closely or well integrated than others). This is especially important for, e.g., lexical analysis — given the assumption made by many linguists that while the grammar (or grammatical meaning) may be structured, the lexicon (or lexical meaning) may not be. How the lexicon is structured, and what similarities and differences between grammatical and lexical structure there are, is a relevant question (basically a problem of the relative autonomy of the lexicon). Seventhly, this means that each item in the linguistic structure has a place and that each place has a value with respect to the overall structure. It is simply not the case that given items are valueless or simply 'intermediate structures' with no direct relationship to the communicative function of language. Nor is any item judged to be more 'basic' than another in terms of their value — each item has a value in terms of the system. Eighthly, a given item is defined by its relation to other items in the system of which it is a part. If in comparing one language with another, we find that given systems (e.g., case systems) are different in terms of their constituent parts, then *a fortiori* both the wholes (the systems themselves) and the parts (the items) are different. Thus, for example, there exists a 'dative' in Russian and a 'dative' in German — but the two are different because the German dative is part of a 4-case system (and thus is coordinated by an accusative, a genitive, and a nominative) while the Russian dative is part of an 8-case system (and thus is related to an accusative, two genitives, a nominative, an instrumental, and two locatives). The German dative and the Russian dative are different items. But even within Russian, Jakobson has shown that across declensions on the formal level the dative is not exactly the same, since not only may it (in conjunction with gender and number) be formally represented by different signantia but also the number of formal oppositions is different in each declension. Jakobson has also provided an example of this with respect to phonology — the phoneme /t/ exists in both Tahitian and Oneidan, but it is essentially different in the two because in Tahitian it is related in the system of stops to /p/ only, whereas in Oneida it is related in the system to /k/ only. Thus, in spite of their phonetic similarity the two /t/'s are linguistically quite different entities, for they obtain their inherent nature not from the sound substance but from the semiotic structure of which they are a part. The /t/ in Tahitian is (−grave) while in Oneida it is (−compact); they are thus not equivalent in spite of their material similarity.

One can, of course, speak about /p/'s in various languages, or case systems in general, focussing on the equivalences without taking account of the differences — but it should be recognized that one is doing just that. A focus on either equivalence or difference is often required in doing linguistic analysis — but it should always be remembered that the two coexist in dialectic tension at any given moment. Finally, this view of structure means that, given the mutual interdependence and mutual interrelationship of all parts of language, from the point of view of the linguistic code, nothing is arbitrary, for each unit has its place in the system and determines the other units and is at the same time determined by them. So, neither the general structure of language itself nor any of its parts is arbitrary. The absolutization of the principle of arbitrariness is, in Jakobson's view, a dangerous exaggeration.

STRUCTURE: PART/WHOLE

Language is, Jakobson claims, a completely hierarchized structure, and one extremely important notion of hierarchical structure is the PART/WHOLE RELATIONSHIP. According to Jakobson, language is itself a relatively autonomous, MULTI-STORIED HIERARCHY OF PARTS AND WHOLES, where the structural laws inherent to the whole determine the nature of the constituent parts and the relationships of the parts to each other and to the whole. (And the parts are always in some sort of hierarchized ('graded') structure *vis-à-vis* each other.) The part/whole hierarchy in language is evidenced in various ways. First of all, language is itself a (relatively autonomous) whole made up of two hierarchized parts — 'phonology' operating with non-semantic constituents of semantic units and grammar and lexicology operating with semantic units. But at the same time, language itself is but part of a larger semiotic whole (overall system of signs) into which it is integrated and which has its own overall characteristics.

This view of language leads to several peculiarities which are particularly important for part/whole relationships.

(1) Each unit can, at one and the same time, be a whole made up of parts and part of a larger whole: this is the notion of *Teilganzes* (SUB-WHOLE or more exactly a PARTIAL WHOLE). In other words, the fact that something is a whole does not preclude on the one hand its being made up of parts and on the other hand its being itself part of a larger whole. Larger wholes, especially above the word level, constitute the matrices which give the various syntactic patterns of a specific language. In such wholes, the parts are in a syntagmatic hierarchy set up by the matrix

itself (e.g., in an attributive matrix, the adjective is subordinate to the noun).

(2) A whole is more than the mechanical sum of its parts: language is not an agglomeration of signs but rather a SYSTEM OF SIGNS, where the relationships of the parts to the whole and of the parts to each other is determined by and determines the structural laws of the whole.

(3) The parts and whole are mutually necessary — the whole cannot exist without its parts and the parts cannot exist without the whole.

(4) The parts of a whole are in some sort of HIERARCHICAL RELATIONSHIP, determined by their place in the whole, that is, by their relation to the other parts. Furthermore, and this is the counterpart of the notion of hierarchy, the parts are not a random set of entities, but exist in a network of interrelations, where each part presupposes every other part and where the subtraction or addition of one part would change the whole and the relationships between the parts as well.

(5) The structural laws inherent to the whole determine whatever happens to any of the constituent parts.

(6) The whole serves as a CONCURRENT CONTEXT for its constituent parts.

The central part/whole relationship in language is the SIGN. Furthermore, the linguistic sign is a sub-whole in the sense that it is at the same time a whole made up of parts and a part of a larger whole (the linguistic system). Thus, the PHONEME is a sub-whole: on the one hand it is a part of larger units (a morpheme or a word — each of which is also a sub-whole) and on the other hand a whole made up of smaller parts called (phonological) DISTINCTIVE FEATURES ('phonological components'). The notion of distinctive features (and of 'componential analysis') is, of course, one of the most important specific insights of Jakobson's into language structure and we will discuss its nature in more detail later. Suffice it to say here, with respect to parts and wholes, that Jakobson has repeatedly warned against mistaking parts of wholes for ULTIMATE CONSTITUENTS. It is clear that while the phoneme is a part, it is not at the same time an ultimate constituent: it is also a whole made up of parts. No meaningful inquiry into phonological structure can be gained without on the one hand recognizing its place in the multistoried hierarchy of parts and wholes making up language and on the other hand decomposing it into its smaller parts, which parts in combination define the unique character of the phoneme. At the same time, the phoneme must be integrated into the morpheme, for the role that a phoneme plays in morphemes not only helps determine and define morphemes but also determines and defines the phoneme itself. In Jakobson's view, the DISTINCTIVE FEATURES are the ultimate constituents of the linguistic code.

Distinctive features are separated into two classes, INHERENT and PROSODIC, depending on whether they rely for their function on opposition or contrast (these two terms will be discussed in more detail later). Both the prosodic and inherent features are divided into three groups (1971i, 33ff.) depending on whether they correspond to one of three main attributes of sensation: INTENSITY, TIME and FREQUENCY. The prosodic features are, furthermore, divided into two varieties of each of the three subclasses, according to whether the frame of reference is either INTERSYLLABIC or INTRASYLLABIC:

The intersyllabic variety of the force features, the STRESS feature, is a contrast of a louder, stressed crest to the less loud, 'unstressed' crests of other syllables within the same sequence.... In the intrasyllabic variety of the stress features, the so-called STOSSTON (stød) feature, two contiguous fractions of the stressed phoneme are compared with each other.... The intersyllabic variety of the quantity features, the LENGTH feature, contrasts a normal, short, unstretchable phoneme within the crest of the syllable with the long, sustained phonemes of the other syllable in the same sequence and/or a normal, short but steady phoneme with a punctual, reduced, transient one.

The second variety of the quantity features, the CONTACT feature, is based on a different distribution of duration between the vowel and the subsequent consonant: in the case of the so-called CLOSE CONTACT (*scharf geschnittener Akzent*), the vowel is abridged in favour of the following, arresting consonant, whereas at the OPEN CONTACT (*schwach geschnittener Akzent*), the vowel displays its full extent before the consonant starts.... In the intersyllabic variety of tone features, which is termed the LEVEL feature, different syllable crests within a sequence are contrasted by their register: higher and lower.... The intrasyllabic variety of tone features, the MODULATION feature, contrasts the higher register of one portion of a phoneme with a lower register of another portion of the same phoneme, or the higher register of one component of a diphthong with the lower register of its other components...." (1971i, 34–5)

Inherent features are subdivided into 8 intensity (=sonority) features: vocalic/non-vocalic, consonantal/non-consonantal, nasal/oral, abrupt/continuant, compact/diffuse, (compact/non-compact, diffuse/non-diffuse), strident/non-strident, checked/unchecked, voice/voiceless; 1 time (=protensity) feature: tense/lax; and 3 frequency (=tonality) features: grave/acute (grave/non-grave, acute/non-acute), flat/non-flat, sharp/non-sharp.[8] Prosodic features depend for their recognition on the "contrast between two variables within one and the same sequence: the RELATIVE voice-pitch, voice-loudness or duration of a given fraction is determined with respect to preceding and/or succeeding fractions" (1971i, 36) while "The recognition and definition of an inherent feature is based only on the choice between two alternatives admissible in the same position within a sequence. No comparison of the two polar terms co-occurring within one context is involved." (1971i, 37–38) The signans of both inherent and prosodic features is thus based on a perceptual characteristic of speech sounds and their signatum, on the 'distinctive' (merely differentiating) function of speech sounds.

In addition to distinctive features, Jakobson has also recognized redundant features which refer to either the concurrent or adjoining context and aid, particularly, in the perception of linguistic units. They also may, in elliptical speech in particular, substitute for the distinctive features (see 1968a — see also my discussion of redundancy above). There are also configurative features (culminative or demarcative) and expressive features (or emphatics) — discussed above.

In parallel to the phoneme, the WORD is also a 'whole' made up of parts — in the word, the parts obtain both for the formal side of the linguistic sign (the phonemes and their respective distinctive features) and for the semantic side of the linguistic sign — the conceptual features. The meaning of a word is not simply a mechanical aggregate of the constituent grammatical, lexical, etc. features — but rather these features themselves interrelate and interact in the 'bundle' making up the meaning. While the combination can be broken up into constituent parts and the parts exist in other bundles elsewhere, it is also the case that the combination itself, because it has a unitary status with respect

[8]There is now, according to Jakobson, even more data on the acoustic and perceptual (i.e. functional) level than on the motor level as to the soundness of this classification. We know now what the necessary elements are that have to be recognized. There is psycho-acoustic data which permit experimental study (e.g. by Delattre 1968). As to terminology, there have been many discussions, but since we know the relations between the different levels, which level the terms are taken from is less important. There are some traditional terms from the motor level; there are terms from the physico-acoustic level (referring to formants, objective phenomena); there are terms like grave/acute, sharp/non-sharp which are common to the physical analysis of musical sounds and of speech sounds. And finally, there are terms such as compact/diffuse, used in psycho-acoustic laboratories such as that of the late S. S. Stevens as characteristic of the interrelations of the formants (see 1951).

to the system, is more than just the sum of those parts. The meaning of a word is itself a whole.[9]

It also cannot be emphasized too strongly here that in the relation of parts to wholes one should not forget the build-up of relationships through the MULTI-LAYERING of the constituent units. The (phonological) distinctive features are only part of the morpheme through the interrelating wholes (phonemes), for the 'bundling' or 'bonding' of the distinctive features into these larger wholes is in itself significant. Similarly, the relationship between the meaning of a phrase and the conceptual features of the constituent parts of the phrase (the words) is not a direct one but rather is mediated by the interrelation of the grammatical, lexical, etc. features in their larger whole — the word — which in turn is only a part of the phrase. Part/whole relationships are highly structured and hierarchized.

One of Jakobson's characterizations of the universal principles of language is done in terms of a necessary, uninvertable hierarchy, which as a rule (in most languages) is composed of the following parts and wholes: DISTINCTIVE FEATURES, PHONEME, SYLLABLE, MORPHEME, WORD, PHRASE, CLAUSE, SENTENCE, UTTERANCE, DISCOURSE are all found in all languages.[10] And indeed he has repeatedly warned against taking one of these to the exclusion of others as the defining characteristic of language; but on the other hand their place in the hierarchical structure of language is extremely important. Furthermore, "each of these ranks is also qualitatively, structurally different" (1955, 233). In particular, each of the wholes is a CONTEXT for its constituent parts: "the word is the context of the morphemes, just as the sentence is the verbal context of words and an utterance the verbal context of sentences, while a morpheme in its turn is the context of phonemes" (1955, 233). This brings out the essentially CONTEXT-SENSITIVE nature of language in terms of part/wholes; it also applies, as we shall see, not only to the discernment of signata but also to the relation between e.g. the message and the non-verbalized context in which it is uttered. Moreover, Jakobson has noted, for example, that there are certain rules of discourse structure which can be discerned and that certain words may depend highly for their interpretation

[9]In much the same way, the dative in Russian is not just the sum of the features of directionality and of marginality, for then it would just be the sum of the accusative and the instrumental. The 'whole' in this case is the combination of the two features and the interaction of the two due to the combination: the whole has its own *Gestaltqualität*.

[10]Although, as mentioned earlier, the relation of morpheme and word is unclear. Similarly, the relation between syllable and morpheme is unclear for those languages which do not seem to differentiate the two.

on the discourse in which they are used. But on the other hand, the difference between a discourse and a word should not be forgotten, and in particular the relatively greater FREEDOM that the speaker has in constructing a sentence and even more so an utterance, than in constructing a new word. In fact, it is a characteristic of the hierarchy of part/whole relationships from the smallest (the distinctive feature) to the largest (discourse) that as one ascends the hierarchy, a comparatively higher degree of freedom is afforded the user of the language, including the freedom to create NOVEL contexts. Furthermore, up through the word, the wholes are codified as units, whereas beyond the word level the wholes are codified only as matrices. And while there are similarities and differences in structure which define the relatively autonomous nature of each of the parts/wholes, it is also the case that at no point in this hierarchy are there any part/wholes which do not have a communicative function.

Jakobson has also repeatedly warned against mistaking parts for wholes in another sense — in not recognizing the fact that a given phenomenon is part of a whole and that its inherent nature cannot be understood without taking cognizance of that fact. (This is, of course, simply another way of viewing relative autonomy plus integration.) ELLIPTICAL SPEECH for example is only one kind of speech and can be understood only in relation to speech in general and in relation to other aspects (sub-codes) of language like explicit speech. Code and message are each constituents of an overall whole and as such neither can be understood without the other. In addition, a given message can only be understood in view of the larger spatio-temporal and situational context in which it is used.

American linguists often talk about 'juncture' phonemes in English. According to Jakobson the phenomenon cannot be formulated solely in terms of phonemes (larger phonological bundles) nor only in terms of strictly distinctive units, but rather in terms of both phonemes and distinctive and demarcative features (the smaller parts). Moreover, the notion 'vowel' is only a subpart of a whole, a name given to a combination of features, specifically the features $\begin{bmatrix} +\text{ vocalic} \\ -\text{ consonantal} \end{bmatrix}$. In like fashion, 'fricative' is not a primitive, but a complex notion, presupposing at least $\begin{bmatrix} +\text{ consonantal} \\ -\text{ vocalic} \\ +\text{ continuant} \\ -\text{ nasal} \end{bmatrix}$. Various cases are considered to be indivisable entities, wholes, but Jakobson has shown that concepts such as 'dative' or 'locative' are actually only complexes, for the dative (in Russian) contains two conceptual features and the locative contains three and furthermore these complexes are parts of a larger whole (the word). Parts of speech are often considered to be wholes, whereas the part of speech nature of a given sign is but one of its defining characteristics, one of its parts. Thus, all prepositions may share certain part of speech features, which then differentiate them from all other parts of speech and these part of speech features 'bundle' with the other features to give the individual prepositions.

Similarly, if we regard signification (the general domain of the signatum) as a part of a whole then it can at the same time be broken down into (interrelated) parts — in particular, the difference between lexicology and grammar. Grammar in its turn is divided into morphology + syntax and morphology may be subdivided (in some languages) into the semantic subclasses of NOMINAL inflection and VERBAL inflection. But to divorce grammatical meaning and lexical meaning completely, as if they had nothing in common, is to forget that both are part of an overall whole — the general domain of meaning. This divorce has led, for example, to a rejection of 'meaning' for such grammatical categories as gender, case, etc. because the 'meaning' of such categories is different from the 'meaning' of concrete nouns like 'house' or 'tree'; and on the other hand, while the tightly knit, hierarchized nature of grammatical systems is recognized, a corresponding patterning for the lexicon is often rejected. However, grammar and lexicology will have equivalences and differences just as for any other relatively autonomous systems of language; and furthermore one can expect to find many transitional types.

Another extremely important concomitant of the part/whole relationship is the notion of *Gestaltqualität* taken over by Jakobson from *Gestalt* psychology and especially from the initiator of this concept, Ehrenfels. The *Gestaltqualität* is the predominant property which characterizes the *Gestalt* (whole) and not the parts of this whole uniquely. The area where this notion has proven most useful is in Jakobson's discussion (see p. 25) of the various functions of language, based on the six parts of any speech situation and the set (focus, orientation, *Einstellung*) of the speaker toward one or the other of these parts.

Other part/whole relationships are discussed in Jakobson's article on parts and wholes (1962c). Furthermore, certain of the antinomies discussed earlier are not only synthesized with respect to the larger whole of which they are a part, but the parts of the antinomies are themselves in a part/whole opposition. One important part mentioned earlier is the SPEECH EVENT, because it can be broken up into constituent parts, and because it is at the same time part of a larger whole — the world of human experience. At the same time, if the speech event is used in deictic categories, then it is part of another larger whole, the narrated event. Thus, the relationship between the parts of the speech event (i.e., between code and message or between message and context), between the parts and the whole (i.e. between the message and the speech event or between the speech event and the world of human experience) is extremely important.

STRUCTURE: OPPOSITION

Thus, one of the major notions of structure, according to Jakobson, is the part/whole relationship and the resultant (inclusion) hierarchy which is produced. But there is another equally relevant notion of hierarchy which is especially important for Jakobson's notion of structure: that built on the relation of the parts to each other. At any given layering of structure, the particular units are, as I said before, interrelated and interconnected. Language then is a NETWORK OF HIERARCHICAL RELATIONS of parts to parts, of parts to wholes, and of wholes to parts.

The most important and the most characteristic relation which exists in language is, according to Jakobson, that of OPPOSITION. In fact, he believes that opposition and invariance (to be discussed later) are two of the most significant and remarkable properties of languages. And he quotes with approval Benveniste who believes in "the dialectic necessity of values in constant opposition as the chief structural principle of language" (1973e, 15). Opposition is in Jakobson's view a relation of MUTUAL AND RECIPROCAL IMPLICATION between two (contrary or contradictory) terms, where each of the terms "univocally, reversibly, and necessarily" (1949f, 421) calls for its definite opposite. Furthermore, neither of the terms can be imagined or thought of without the other, opposite term: "The presence of one term of a binary opposition necessarily implies and educes the other, opposite term". (1962b, 637) The existence of one necessarily implies, and gives predictable information about, the existence of the other. Examples of opposition are, in the domain of phonology, nasal/oral, long/short; in the domain of grammar, plural/singular, feminine/masculine; in the domain of the lexicon, cheap/expensive, ugly/beautiful. The concept of opposition is essentially different from that of a 'contingent duality' "where neither of the two members can predict something about the other one (see Pos)" (1968a, 709). As Jakobson points out, the mutual implication inherent to the notion of opposition makes language a much more efficient tool and aids both in the perception of speech and in the acquisition of language by children, whereas a contingent duality is much more inefficient.

Opposition is also different from the notion of CONTRAST:

> The term *contrast* is usually employed to denote a juxtaposition and comparison of two simultaneous or successive stimuli, contiguous in perception. These two stimuli are mutually influenced in the direction of increasing their apparent difference; but the existence of one does not imply the existence of the other. On the contrary, two opposites necessarily imply each other if, in the given span of perception, only one of them is present. (1951, 442)

House and *cent* may, because of 'juxtaposition and comparison' be in a relation of contrast in a given situation, but they do not form an opposition. Moreover, PROSODIC FEATURES depend, for their recognition, on the contrast within the sequence, and the relative position of the two opposing components. "Thus both alternatives of a prosodic feature coexist in the code as two terms of an opposition and moreover, co-occur and produce a contrast within the message." (1971i, 37) Inherent features, on the other hand, are not only oppositional in terms of the code but also depend for their recognition and definition minimally on the choice between two alternatives; no assumption is made that the two alternatives will occur in a given sequence. This does not mean, of course, that inherent features may not be influenced by the context — assimilation, dissimilation, etc. occur and produce the redundancy which make the perception of speech more efficient.

Not all relations in language are relations of opposition and this is particularly true of vocabulary according to Jakobson: the word *house* seems to have no clearly discernable opposite.[11] Most proper names have no clearly definable and predictable opposite. On the other hand, the notion of opposition underlies and defines PHONOLOGY and GRAMMAR. In fact, phonology and grammar may be differentiated in terms of opposition coupled with the concept of the linguistic sign: "in the former case (phonological opposition) the coupled contradictories reside in the perceptible side of language (signans or 'signifier'), whereas

[11] Van Schooneveld (MS) has however postulated that lexical items can be analyzed in terms of opposition if we apply the term on the feature level. In fact, he has discerned a hierarchy of the conceptual features based on the principle of mutual implication.

in the latter (grammatical opposition) they lie in its intelligible side (signatum or 'signified')." (1972a, 78)

The concept of opposition and of TWO POLAR OPPOSITES is a mutually implicating one. One cannot have an opposition (e.g. quantity) without having at the same time the two polar opposites — long vs. short. And likewise, one cannot have the opposition of two polar opposites (long vs. short) without having at the same time an overriding PRINCIPIUM which units the two (e.g. quantity). So, the two terms employed by Fischer-Jörgensen (1975) ('dimension' vs. 'components') are mutually implicating and the use of one of the components (e.g. 'long') for the whole dimension ('the quantity opposition' or 'the quantity feature') is justified because of the mutual predictability, although it would be clearer if the dimension were elegantly separated from the opposites.

According to Jakobson, the notion of two polar opposites in any given opposition is inherent to the notion of opposition: to call an opposition a binary one is a tautology. The binary nature of opposition and the BINARISM inherent in Jakobson's view of language have been attacked from various points of view, but it should be pointed out that binarism is, in Jakobson's view, not a concept imposed on language, but rather derived from the nature of language.[12] He has defended it on numerous occasions (see in particular 1956a; 1961b; 1971i) in terms of efficiency and optimality (discussed above), of its evident usefulness in communication theory, of its early appearance in the child ("the pair is anterior to the isolated object"), of the patently binary nature of certain oppositions (e.g. nasal–oral) and of its overwhelming usefulness in typology, laws of implication, and structuring of phonemic systems. (I will discuss binarism in more detail later, with respect to markedness.) In addition, with respect to ternary relationships, we should take our past experience as extremely important. It was often said in phonology for example, that the stops /p/-/t/-/k/ are aligned in a three-term relationship which cannot be reduced to a binary one. But Jakobson has shown (e.g., through the earlier acquisition of the opposition *p/t*

[12]Furthermore, as he is fond of saying, we may in the Brazilian jungle find a language which uses non-binary relationships, just as we might find a five-legged cat — but it is important to know that that is highly unusual. It does not invalidate our saying that language is essentially binary or that cats are essentially four-legged. On a more serious level, just as the biologists have found, in Australia, mammals which lay eggs (the duck-billed platypus, echidna), and just as this has caused a redefinition of mammals, yet it has not led biologists to say that mammals are not, in general, non-egg-laying. Again, it is essential to know that it is unusual to find an egg-laying mammal — or a language which is non-binary (1953c; 1963a).

and the later acquisition of *p-t/k* in children) that /k/ is opposed to both /p/ and /t/ as (+compact) vs. (−compact), while the /p/ and /t/ are opposed to each other as (+grave) vs. (−grave). The seeming equality of the three was only illusory. Similarly, in the wide-spread system of the so-called three 'personal pronouns', the first and second person pronouns are opposed to the third as participants in the speech event, while the first person is opposed to the second person as the producer of the given message. So the seeming equality necessarily breaks down into a double opposition. And if one takes the tenses of French, there is a seeming tripartite division between past, present, and future. But again, a systematic look at the information conveyed shows (Waugh 1976c; see also 1957a; 1959d) that the present is unmarked (a zero category) opposed on the one hand to the imperfect and on the other hand to the future. Being each marked by a different feature and having at the same time no marking in common leads to the fact that, when used to refer to the time axis, the imperfect and the future seem to be the 'opposites' of one another. But the fact that the markings themselves are not 'opposite' is clear because they also combine to form the conditional.

Another extremely important point about the nature of opposition in language, and one which Jakobson has discussed while showing that Saussure had not carried his own principle to its ultimate conclusion (1939a; 1971d; 1973e), is that one must apply the notion of opposition to the right level of structure, to the right units. As he has repeatedly pointed out, to say that /p/ is bilabial in opposition to /t/, which in turn is dental in opposition to velar /k/ is to apply the notion of opposition at the wrong level. A bilabial /p/ does not imply or necessitate the presence of the dental /t/ or velar /k/ (as the Tahitian and Oneidan examples discussed earlier show). The whole /p/ is opposed to and thus related to the whole /t/ only in terms of their CONSTITUENT PARTS — and these constituent parts are in an oppositional relation. If [+grave] is used in a given linguistic system to define a phoneme or a set of phonemes then by necessity there is also [−grave] in the same system to define a phoneme or a set of phonemes. The presence of [+grave] as an OPPOSITIONAL COMPONENT necessarily entails the presence of [−grave] as its opposite. Thus, the use of [+grave] in a particular system implies the use of [−grave] in that same system and vice versa: the oppositional relation of the features +grave/−grave is then characteristic of the given system and is used to differentiate some if not all of the phonemes of that system. Thus, such phonological correlations as *p*:*b*::*t*:*d*::*k*:*g*::*f*:*v*::*s*:*z*::*š*:*ž* are very revealing, because they show that the importance of the proportions lies not in the phonemes cited but in the common opposition being brought into focus (in this case either +tense/−tense or −voice/+voice depending on the language). Such binary oppositions are defined "par un principe commun qui peut être pensé indépendamment de chaque couple de termes opposés" (1928b, 3).

Likewise, the dative and locative in the Russian case system are opposed one to the other in terms of their oppositional characteristics — the whole 'dative' is opposed to the whole 'locative' only in terms of their constituent parts. And the presence of [+directionality] as a grammatical feature for the dative implies and necessitates the presence of [Ø directionality] in the case system as a grammatical feature (e.g., the nominative and instrumental are both unmarked for directionality). And so on.

Oppositions, then, in phonology and grammar, are given most generally in terms of features (phonological or grammatical minima): the essential relationships between units is provided by the OPPOSITIONAL FEATURES in a mutually implicating relationship. Since two units may share some features and not share others, units may be more or less different or more or less the same; there may be certain equivalences between items, but there are always differences.

We have seen then that opposition implies the presence of two mutually implicating polar opposites. These opposites are not, however, in an equal relationship *vis-à-vis* each other: rather they are in the unequal (hierarchized) relationship given by markedness — one of the terms is marked and the other is unmarked. In fact, as far as Jakobson is concerned, the notion of MARKEDNESS follows just as naturally from the notion of opposition as does binarism. Fully seen, an opposition is a mutually implicating and predicting relationship between two polar opposites of which one is marked and the other is unmarked. Furthermore, their status *vis-à-vis* each other, as well as *vis-à-vis* the dimension given by the opposition, is (relationally) invariant. The marking itself is relationally invariant in terms of the opposition as a whole and in terms of the other oppositions present in the system. Thus, the notion of markedness, besides being a defining characteristic of the principle of opposition, is built essentially and inherently on the notion of RELATIONAL INVARIANCE. But relational invariance is actually more widespread than its application to opposition: it is relational rather than oppositional. So I will discuss here, before going on to markedness, the principle of relational invariance.

RELATIONAL INVARIANCE

As was pointed out earlier, relational invariance is one of the three keystones of Jakobson's science of language — deriving its essential characteristics from, and providing essential characteristics for, the importance of relations and particularly the relation of opposition (and the concomitant notions of marked/unmarked) on the one hand and on the other hand the separation of the more general signans from its more specific, contextually determined implementations and of the more general signatum from its more specific, contextually determined interpretations.

The principle of invariance, simply stated, says that there is associated with any item in any language certain defining characteristics which remain no matter what alterations of or influences on that item there may be as it is used in various contexts or situations. From the absolute phonetic point of view no two sounds are strictly identical — each replication of a sound is different from every other. Moreover, even if we 'factor out' those differences which are not perceivable by the human ear, from the absolute phonetic point of view there is an amazing multitude of sounds produceable by and discernable by speakers of a given language. But from the point of view of the linguistic system in which they are used, certain of the sounds are considered to be identical (there is a certain EQUIVALENCE between them which overrides the perceivable differences) while others are considered to be non-identical. The "EQUIVALENCE IN DIFFERENCE" (1959a, 262) is the invariance associated with the various sounds through the linguistic system of which they are a part. Invariance is a product of the linguistic system, is a creation of language through its semiotic status. This is particularly evident in grammar and lexicon for invariance in this domain may have little to do with absolute affinities of the referents involved (if referents there be) but with imputed similarities and differences from the point of view of the linguistic system. They may be LINGUISTIC FICTIONS which are nevertheless extremely real to the speakers of the given language and can create a whole 'mythology' for those speakers. Furthermore, they are not shocking, since they are firmly rooted in and define to a certain extent the whole conceptual framework. They may, however, exist only in terms of the linguistic system of which they are a part and may appear from the point of view of another linguistic system to be arbitrary and ad hoc. It is well known that given languages do not classify the world in the same way. Invariance in general and the given invariants are not however *ad hoc* and arbitrary for the speakers of a given language — they are, rather, necessary and completely logical from a linguistic point of view.

RELATIONAL INVARIANCE, again simply stated, means that these defining characteristics adhere in the item itself only in so far as it is related to other items of the system of which it is a part. Since the relations are primary and the items themselves secondary, so the invariance itself of those items is primarily relational. Invariance is built on and implies the notion of relation (and in fact, according to Jakobson, can be understood only in connection with the notion of relations). As Jakobson has pointed out (1973e) the 1870's in mathematics and in linguistics (the Kazan' school — 1943, 1960d) had shown the importance of the notion of invariance, but it was not until the early part of the twentieth century, with the advent of the theory of relativity and its emphasis on relations as primary and invariance as dependent upon the relations themselves, that the very fruitful notion of relational invariance could be understood. This was a very difficult step at the time—and while the notion of relational invariance has been recognized in linguistics for a good part of the 20th century, it has been a step which has not been fully taken by all. To go back to the example quoted before, *house* has its invariant defining characteristics only by virtue of the fact that it is related to (and thus equivalent to in some respects and different from in other respects) other buildings, from the standpoint of the English language. Relational invariance, in its linguistic aspect, then, is built on certain RELATIONAL PROPERTIES which items of human experience have in common from the point of view of the linguistic system, and which they possess only as they are related to other items of human experience.[13]

Relational invariance is, according to Jakobson (1972a; 1973e), the cornerstone of language and linguistics. It is found everywhere, from the largest unit down to the smallest, in the relationship between any coordinated parts and their wholes, in the antinomies which are characteristic of language. Moreover, this principle underlies not only other semiotic systems, but also cognate disciplines such as biology, physics, mathematics, etc. And topology, of course, is the science of invariance.

[13]I will remind the reader here that the world of human experience is not equal to ontological reality and that this 'world' is essentially correlated with language.

It is true, of course, that one would hardly find a serious linguist who does not work with some notion of invariance (hardly any linguist today would say that each and every item in each and every message is unique; in fact invariance is a necessary concomitant of the dichotomy code/message), but what differentiates Jakobson's thought from that of other linguists is not only the fact that he considers that language is based consistently on the principle of relational invariance, but also the way in which he thinks invariance is actually realized in language, and, in addition, the consistency with which the principle is applied methodologically.

Relational invariance, then, is 'EQUIVALENCE UNDER ISOMORPHIC TRANSFORMATIONS': relational invariants are specific properties which are not necessarily affected by a modification of the absolute data upon which they rest. Some phonological and grammatical equivalences may be given in the form of PROPORTIONS. In this way we can say that *p*:*b*::*t*:*d*::*k*:*g*, where *p*, *t*, *k* are all equivalent in terms of their differentiation from *b*, *d*, *g* respectively, in terms of a given distinctive feature. In like manner *p*, *b*, *f*, *v*, *m* are equivalent with respect to one of their defining properties, and so are *p*, *b*, *f*, *v*, *m*, *u*, *ɨ*. Similarly, in grammar such proportions as *boy*:*boys*::*hat*:*hats*, *catch*:*caught*::*bring*:*brought* or *able*:*ability*::*capable*:*capability* are commonplace. Furthermore, one can set up the proportions (Russian) nominative: instrumental::accusative:dative, (English) *in*:*out*::*on*:*off*::*at*:*from*, (French) present:imperfect::future:conditional; moreover, such statements as 'the nominative (accusative) occupies the same place in the case system as *na* (*po*) in the prepositional system of Russian" (Van Schooneveld, MS) have a meaning, but only if seen in the light of equivalence.

If a given item is said to evidence a particular relational invariant, then it must be the case that wherever that item is used, the invariant is present. If a /p/ in a particular language is defined as $\begin{bmatrix} +\text{ consonantal} \\ -\text{ vocalic} \\ -\text{ nasal} \\ -\text{ compact} \\ +\text{ grave} \\ -\text{ continuant} \\ +\text{ tense} \end{bmatrix}$,

then it is because all instances of /p/ are characterized by those RELATIONAL QUALITIES. In other words, if [−voice] were to be distinctive for

/p/ in English, the /p/ would have to be unvoiced in all its occurrences. (In fact, /p/ is not always [−voice] due to assimilation in consonant clusters; /p/ is invariantly [+tense] as against the [−tense]/b/.) If /k/ in English is said to be 'velar' ($\begin{bmatrix} +\text{ compact} \\ +\text{ grave} \end{bmatrix}$), then it must always be invariantly velar. But in fact it is not. /k/ is only [+compact] in opposition to /p/ and /t/; it is not in addition [+grave] for /k/ is more front before front vowels and more back before back vowels. Similarly, with respect to grammatical categories, if the imperfect in French is assumed to be marked for [+past time], then everywhere it is used it must categorize in some way past time. But in fact, this is not so — the imperfect in French refers to both past time (*il pleuvait hier*) as well as to irreal situations (*s'il pleuvait maintenant*) at the present time. An invariant exists for these two uses (Waugh 1976c) but that invariant is not [+past time]. Reference to past time is only a contextual variant (but perhaps the major contextual variant) of the feature characteristic of the imperfect.

In Jakobson's view ALL DIFFERENCES HAVE A FUNCTION, but certain differences are distinctive ones (e.g., the differences between /p/ and /b/ in English) while other differences are redundant ones (e.g., the differences between [p] and [p^{h}] in English). The latter is also an example of equivalence in difference on the one hand and of the opposition between the invariant (the phoneme /p/) and its contextual variants ([p] and [p^{h}]) on the other hand. Furthermore, if we take, for example, pairs of active and passive sentences in English, certain equivalences can be noted in terms of the agent/patient relationship (e.g. 'natives hunt lions'/'lions are hunted by natives'), but the differences between them in terms of subject function as against prepositional phrase are also important. Moreover, if we take such constructions as 'he read the book' and 'he read all day', in terms of modification, the two phrases *the book* and *all day* are equivalent — they both modify the verb *read* directly (i.e., without the intermediary of a preposition). On the other hand, a large difference in interpretation of the relationship between *the book* or *all day* and *read* exists –which difference, given the intimate connection between form and meaning, is due to the differences in the lexical items involved. The grammatical (syntactic) constructions are the same. This all shows, as Jakobson has often pointed out, that equivalences are important — but it must not be forgotten that there is only equivalence in difference.

Invariance/Variation

The relational invariance of an item is to be differentiated from the multitude of VARIATION which that item may exhibit as it is used in various CONTEXTS and situations. The invariant is generic in nature and is determined by the relational system of which it is part; the variants are more SPECIFIC and determined in addition by the context of which they are a part. This points up in particular the CONTEXT-SENSITIVE nature of language. There is a relation of mutual dependency between the invariant and the variants for on the one hand the invariant cannot exist without variation; and on the other hand variants have a status as variants only *vis-à-vis* the related invariant. Moreover, there is a hierarchical arrangement of the contextual variants — most specifically in terms of a BASIC meaning (i.e., that which the sign has out of context) vs. the PERIPHERAL meaning (i.e., that which the sign has in context), and this hierarchy of the parts attests to the reality of the complex whole. There is an almost limitless range of contextual variants and new contextual variants are created as new situations arise — and both the creation of new contexts for old words by speakers, and their understanding by addressees, attests not only to the reality of the invariant but also to its inherent nature.

Variants are to a large extent CONTEXTUAL and/or STYLISTIC:

> Transformations that provide the invariants (distinctive features) with diverse concomitant variations can be roughly divided into two kinds of alternation: contextual and stylistic. Contextual variants point to the concurrent or consecutive neighborhood of the given feature, whereas stylistic variants add a marked — emotive or poetic — annex to the neutral, purely cognitive information of the distinctive feature. (1972a, 77).

An example of invariance/variation is the distinctive feature opposition sharp-plain in Russian: "The upward shift of pitch remains an unaltered invariant mark of the Russian consonantal opposition sharp/plain, whatever are its varying implementations conditioned by combination with different concurrent and/or subsequent features (higher spectral level at least in one of the consonantal phases or an i-like formant transition to the following vowel)." (1968a, 712) An example of invariance/variation in lexical meaning is Jakobson's analysis of the word *bachelor* in English where the (contextual) variants are those noted by other scholars who have also analyzed this word: "(1) adult man, but unmarried, (2) academic degree, but the lowest, (3) knight, but without a banner of his own, (4) adult seal, but without a mate during breeding time" (1972b, 50). Jakobson has discerned, behind the multitude of variation, the invariant: all the bachelors have it in common that they are all adult males (except when there is categorial indication of the context to the contrary — e.g. 'bachelor girl') and with one item in their career which remains incomplete (cf. 1972b, 50). But of course, Jakobson has studied most extensively the antinomy invariance/variation in the domain of grammar. Thus, the invariant ('intension', general meaning) for the accusative case in Russian is 'directionality' whereas its contextual variants ('extension', actual application of the case) include the 'direct object' of a transitive verb ('to write *a letter*'), 'a segment of space or time entirely filled by the action' ('to live *a year*', 'to go *the whole way*'), the object of certain prepositions with 'directedness' implications ('onto *the table*'), etc. (1936; 1958b).

But such invariants, while they are put into relation with their corresponding contextual variants, must also be put in relation with (and in some cases in opposition to) other invariants in order for the relational invariant to be fully understood. Thus, for example, the feature of 'directionality' and the accusative case it defines can be fully understood only in terms of the case system as a whole.

It cannot be emphasized too strongly that both the invariant and the variants are from Jakobson's point of view part of the linguistic system. On the one hand, the invariants are not, as others have said, abstract or fictitious entities imposed on the data by the linguist, but are in fact 'CODE-GIVEN TRUTHS' (1962b, 650) which are actually present in the diverse variants:

Le phonème n'est ni identique au son ni extérieur par rapport au son, mais il est nécessairement présent dans le son, il lui demeure inhérent et superposé: c'est *l'invariant dans les variations*. (1939d, 315)

And the invariant qualities of speech sounds have been given support by neurophysiological research on perception:

Contemporary research on the neurophysiological foundations of perception places particular stress on "the role of central factors in perception" and on the "centrally-induced control of sense data", as Bruner states. His illuminating study on neural mechanisms in perception adduces "the categorial nature of perceptual identification", and points out that "the equivalence of stimulus events is a function of certain invariances in relationship". In our perceptual faculty "we come to identify constances, treating as equivalent objects that have been altered drastically in all respects save their defining attributes". (1968a, 707)

Perhaps the best data for the reality of grammatical and lexical invariants, besides the categorial nature of percepts and concepts, is the CREATION of new contextual variants (new contexts) for morphemes, words, phrases, etc., which contextual variants are understood and interpreted by the addressee even though he may never have met them before. The ability on the part of the speaker to create and on the part of the hearer to apprehend new contextual variants attests to the reality and productivity of the invariants in the code. Such new creations are, of course, very prevalent in poetic discourse: the poet makes use of new possibilities of contextual modifications of the general meaning associated with given items. Thus the poetic use of language, far from being deviant, rather makes use of secondary, contextual meanings of the general invariant meaning of a given sign.[14] Poetic usage is part of language in general, and should not be ignored in doing an analysis of linguistic structure. But we must not forget that in ordinary discourse, despite the multitude of stereotyped expressions and hackneyed phrases, creative, especially figurative, usage is also found. Such usage can be explained only by the reality of the invariant in the system.

In like fashion the variants (contextual and stylistic) are also linguistically determined — variation is not unbounded or completely free because ultimately the invariant (no matter how different it might appear to be) must be present in all the variations. Thus, for instance, contextual meanings are due to the use of given words in verbalized and/or non-verbalized but verbalizable contexts. Even figurative (METAPHORICAL and METONYMIC) uses are determined by the invariant in question, for metaphorical usage is in a relation of similarity and metonymic usage in a relation of contiguity with the invariant in question. Creativity is, of course, possible, but creativity is associated with a specific linguistic system.

Invariance: Linguistic Sign

Relational invariance is also the integrating property of the LINGUISTIC SIGN as a whole. A linguistic sign is, according to Jakobson, a combination of a signans which is relationally invariant with a signatum, which likewise is relationally invariant, where the invariant signans and the invariant signatum are more general than and to be differentiated from

[14] Much the same point is made by Sangster in the manuscript mentioned in footnote 8, p. 22.

their contextual variations. Furthermore, both the signans and the signatum may be invariant wholes made up of parts which themselves are invariant. If we speak of the phoneme, the signans is actually an invariant bundle of invariant concurrent distinctive features while the signatum is 'mere otherness'. If we speak of the word, the largest linguistic sign to be codified as such, then the signans is made up of an invariant sequence of invariant phonemes, while the signatum is itself an invariant, a larger whole (a 'bundle') made up of invariant concurrent lexical and grammatical features. For each invariant of meaning there is a concomitant and associated invariant of form. I have characterized this above as the 'one form-one meaning' principle (see p. 46), although 'one meaning-one form' would be better due to the possibility of homonymy. From this has come an extremely important methodological criterion:[15] in general, in linguistic methodology, we go from form to meaning or, at least, if we approach a language knowing what concepts are distinguished (formally) in other languages, we may search for those which are formally differentiated, on the one hand, and on the other hand, we are ever ready to seek out the meaning correlates for the formal differences which a language provides. The relevant question, then, is 'how is the meaning supported by the form'. There is a direct relationship between the signans and the signatum; for every invariant signans there is at least one invariant signatum (or more, in cases of homonymy). The form then is partially deterministic from the methodological point of view (from the linguistic point of view both form and meaning are mutually deterministic) — the form shows the investigator where (but not what) the meaning categories of a language are. Furthermore, the only way to know whether or not homonymy exists for a given form is to show first that there is no 'common denominator' behind the various uses. This is extremely important — otherwise, homonyms may be posited at will and in an arbitrary fashion.

Relational Invariance: Signans

Relational invariance is most extensively operative and yet least understood in the relationship between the features, whether distinctive or conceptual, and their various contextual manifestations, and in the interaction of the features themselves. If we take the distinctive features,

[15] See 1949e; 1953c; 1971c for statements to this effect, as well as Sangster 1970.

then Jakobson has long claimed that absolute differences between various material manifestations (particularly articulatory ones) are not relevant, if the given material manifestations are themselves never in opposition. Thus, since labialization, pharyngealization, retroflexion, etc. are never in opposition (i.e., either only one of them occurs in a given language or within one language one may occur with one set of sounds and the other may occur with a different set — there is complementary distribution either across languages or, in a given language, with respect to a given concurrent context), and since both have a similar acoustic property and perceptual effect, they are, from the point of view of the linguistic system, contextual variants of the general (relational) invariant flat/non-flat. The invariant definable for flat/non-flat is relative to the particular acoustic and articulatory manifestation of the feature, both of which are in turn relative to the particular system or even to the particular terms of the system in which they are used.

Another example of relational invariance is the famous Danish dental consonants quoted frequently by Jakobson. This one is particularly important for it shows that what may, from the acoustician's point of view, be the same sound in two different positions is not the same at all from the point of view of the linguistic system. In Danish, [t] and [d] occur in initial position in the word, while [d] and [đ] occur in medial position. Leaving aside the inventory of sounds and concentrating on the oppositions relevant in each position, we see that Danish has an opposition tense/lax in both positions, but the tense phoneme is implemented by a [t] in one position and by a [d] in the other:

	initial	medial
/t/ tense	t	d
/d/ lax	d	đ

(1949f, 424)

Similar to this is the Old Gilyak system of compact consonants:

Phoneme	Position Strong	Weak
Strong /k'/	k'	k
Weak /k/	k	x

(1975d, 95)

In other words, in the two languages, there is a general weakening of sounds in medial as against initial position. This means that the tense phoneme is weaker in medial position than in initial position, but that at the same time the lax phoneme is weaker in medial position than in initial position, so that the relative position of the tense as against the lax phoneme is the same. This also means that [d], [k] implement two different phonemes, or the two phonemes 'overlap' in [d], [k] if looked at from the absolute point of view. But if looked at from the relationally invariant point of view of the linguistic system, the exact phonetic manifestation is not important. What is important is the relative position of the sounds, and the relationally invariant opposition. From this point of view the two *d*'s, two *k*'s are not the same.

Another example akin to this one comes from French (1949d): there are two mid front unrounded vowels in the phonemic system, the tense /ê/, implemented by [e] in open syllables and [ɛ:] in closed syllables, and the lax /e/ implemented by [ɛ] in both types of syllables. Although [ɛ:] and [ɛ] may be more similar in terms of vowel quality than are [e] and [ɛ:], it is clear that in terms of oppositions the /ê/ is always more tense (either higher — [e] — or longer — [ɛ:]) than the lax /e/ (lower and/or shorter — [ɛ]). This example also points up another attribute of the principle of relational invariance: oppositions are most often set up in terms of more vs. less (i.e. more tension vs. less tension) rather than in terms of absolutes.

A further example of relational invariance, which again shows that the relations are primary and that the relative positions of the terms of the oppositions, rather than their absolute positions, are most important, is the Gilyak vocalic system (1957d, 82) (the Bulgarian vocalic system is the same — 1962b, 642):

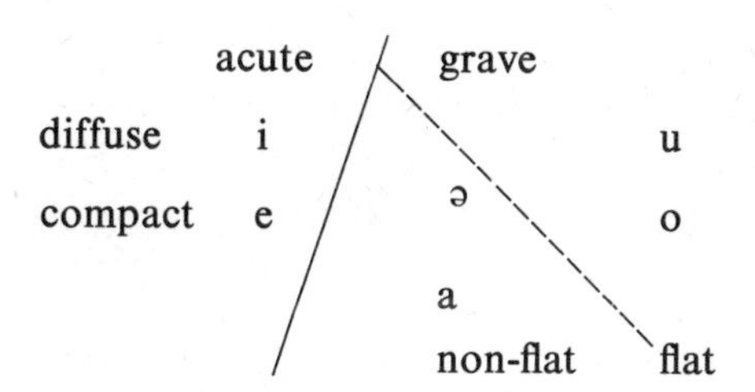

where the diffuse/compact opposition is implemented by /i/-/e/, /ə/-/a/, /u/-/o/. Thus /ə/ is relatively more diffuse than the compact /a/, even though in terms of its absolute position, it is almost as low as /e/ and /o/, which are both compact. Furthermore, there is an essential difference between the /e/ of Gilyak (or of Bulgarian) and the /e/ of French: the former is compact, because it is opposed only to /i/; the latter is non-compact, non-diffuse because it is opposed to both /i/ and /a/; furthermore, it is [+flat] being opposed to /ϕ/ and [−tense] being opposed to /ê/.

Further examples show that not only must one operate with the phonetic relations and the interrelations within the system, but also one must ask how the features are combined in a given bundle: features are invariant with respect to their concurrent context.[16] Thus, for instance, in French (1949d) [+compact] in the consonantal system is implemented by a palatal /ñ/ when combined with [+nasal], by palato-alveolar /š/, /ž/ when combined with $\begin{bmatrix}-\text{nasal}\\+\text{continuant}\end{bmatrix}$ and by post-palatal /k/, /g/ when combined with $\begin{bmatrix}-\text{nasal}\\-\text{continuant}\end{bmatrix}$. Although the implementations are different, the relational invariance of the feature [+compact] remains the same: it is always further back than the alveolar region. The tense/lax opposition is also implemented in various ways, depending on whether it is used in the vowels or consonants, and within the vowels whether it is combined with [+compact], [+diffuse] or $\begin{bmatrix}-\text{compact}\\-\text{diffuse}\end{bmatrix}$. In the consonants (i.e., in segments marked $\begin{bmatrix}+\text{consonantal}\\-\text{vocalic}\end{bmatrix}$), [+tense]–[−tense] defines the oppositions /p/-/b/,/t/-/d, /k/-/g/, /f/-/v/, /s/-/z/, /š/-/ž/ (voicing is not distinctive in French because it is assimilated in consonant clusters). In the [+diffuse] vowels (i.e. in the simultaneous environment of $\begin{bmatrix}+\text{vocalic}\\-\text{consonantal}\\+\text{diffuse}\end{bmatrix}$) [+tense]—[−tense] opposes /i/ and /y/, /u/ and /w/, /ü/ and /ẅ/ (/y/, /w/ and /ẅ/ are not true glides because they have a formant structure and do not have low total energy). In the [+compact] vowels, tense/lax opposes /â/ to /a/, where the opposition is sometimes implemented as back/front ([ɑ]/[a]), sometimes as long/short ([a:]/[a]), sometimes as a combination of these ([ɑ:]/[a]). In the $\begin{bmatrix}-\text{compact}\\-\text{diffuse}\end{bmatrix}$ vowels, tense/lax opposes the higher mid to lower mid vowels (i.e. [e]/[ɛ], [o]/[ɔ], [ϕ]/[œ]) although (as we saw in the dis-

[16]This is of course due in part to the fact that the whole is more than the sum of the parts and provides an overall structure for an understanding of the given parts. Furthermore, the 'bundling' or 'bonding' of the parts into the whole is relevant.

cussion earlier of /ê/ and /e/) the tense vowel can be lower mid when it is lengthened ([ɛ:]/[ɛ]).

Perhaps the most general examples of relational invariance come from the extremely important opposition of consonants $\begin{bmatrix} +\text{consonantal} \\ -\text{vocalic} \end{bmatrix}$ to vowels $\begin{bmatrix} -\text{consonantal} \\ +\text{vocalic} \end{bmatrix}$. The vast majority of the distinctive features apply to both consonants and vowels, but have a quite different implementation in each. The grave/acute opposition (1956a), for example, divides the low tonality from the high tonality phonemes. In the consonants, the low tonality phonemes are genetically peripheral — either labial or velar — while the high tonality phonemes are medial — dental or palatal; in the vowels, the low tonality phonemes are the peripheral (velar or 'back') vowels while the high tonality phonemes are the medial ('front') vowels. It is thus understandable that /p/ and /k/ are related to /u/, and /t/ and /c/ are related to /i/.

Another example of the importance of the simultaneous environment is stridency in the [+consonantal] phonemes. In combination with $\begin{bmatrix} -\text{vocalic} \\ -\text{continuant} \end{bmatrix}$ the strident/non-strident opposition generally relates affricates to stops in the pre-velar region (/c/ vs. /t/, /č/ vs. /ç/, /pf/ vs. /p/), whereas for the $\begin{bmatrix} +\text{compact} \\ (+\text{grave}) \\ -\text{continuant} \end{bmatrix}$ phonemes it relates uvulars to velars; in combination with $\begin{bmatrix} +\text{vocalic} \\ -\text{continuant} \end{bmatrix}$ it relates e.g. Czech /ř/ to /r/. For $\begin{bmatrix} -\text{vocalic} \\ +\text{continuant} \end{bmatrix}$ phonemes the relevant opposition is generally the so-called strident fricatives as against their mellow counterparts (/s/ vs. /θ/, /f/ vs. /φ/ while for $\begin{bmatrix} +\text{vocalic} \\ +\text{continuant} \end{bmatrix}$ it distinguishes /ł/ from /l/. The absolute phonetic implementations of the strident/non-strident opposition are varied — but the relationally invariant nature of the opposition remains: the higher intensity noise of the strident phoneme as against the lower intensity noise of its mellow counterpart.

Another consequence of the notion of relational invariance is that once the points of the system are established with respect to their relationship to all other points, then the range of variation within the invariance is to a large extent determined. It has been pointed out that in French (1949d) there is only one [+compact] nasal consonant. Now, normally the consonant is implemented by /ñ/; but given the fact that the grave/acute opposition is redundant, other realizations such as /ŋ/ are possible and, as Jakobson noted in referring to Sweet's work (1949d, 428–9), have been observed in spoken French. In a related way, the stops p/b, t/d, k/g in English are opposed as tense/lax with unvoiced/voiced as a redundant counterpart. Given this, it is not surprising that in certain combinations of consonants, as well as in medial position, the normally unvoiced tense consonants may become voiced and yet not merge with their lax (normally voiced) counterparts, because the tense/lax opposition is maintained.

Relational Invariance: Signatum

Examples of relational invariance in the signatum are clearly different from those in phonology, given the fact that the relational invariance pertains to the conceptual features[17] rather than to the distinctive features. (I reiterate here that the invariant of meaning is on the one hand generic and on the other hand separate from reference.) A very obvious example, paralleling the different status of [d] in Danish in terms of its categorization, is that the same situation may be categorized in different ways (and talked about using different words) by the given linguistic system: "A difference in grammatical concepts does not necessarily represent a difference in the state of affairs referred to." (1968b, 598) Thus, the active vs. the passive voice may refer to the same action but focus on and give importance to different participants; *buy* and *sell* can be used for the same situation but focus differently on the direction in which the exchange takes place; one can say *he's at the house* and *he's in the house* referring to the same event, but *at* and *in* categorize the situation differently (in particular, *in* is more specific than *at*); *woman* and *female human being* can have the same referent but the latter provides more information explicitly and uses separate words; *Napoleon captured Paris in 1808* and *Napoleon captures Paris in 1808* refer to the same event but the distinction between the past and the present tense is still relevant; there are 'tautological' objects in both the instru-

[17]In what follows we will be discussing various grammatical and lexical categories in diverse languages. But, just as in phonology, it is assumed that the features used to define those categories form a system (see in particular van Schooneveld MS). They are thus not as unrelated as they may appear to be at first glance (see footnote 26, p. 99).

mental and the accusative in Russian, where the difference is the way in which the object is viewed *vis-à-vis* the verbal process and not necessarily anything inherent in the objects themselves (1936; 1958b). And so on. Again, it is not a question of the absolute material manifestation which is important, but rather of how this reality is viewed in terms of linguistic categorization. It is well known that different human beings can look at the same situation and focus on it and describe it in different ways, and these different ways really reflect different perceptions. That this should also be represented in language is not surprising.

For a cross-language view of relational invariance, one may say that English *in*, French *en*, Russian *v* are all marked with roughly the same conceptual feature. But the relational invariance of the feature itself is different in all three cases because the overall system is different: *in* in English is related to e.g. *at*, *on*, *by*, *to*, etc., whereas *en* in French is related to e.g., *à*, *de*, *dans*, *par*, etc., while Russian v is related to e.g. *na*, *za*, *po*, etc. In each case, the range of situations for which the given preposition is used is different — and this is due to the fact that the pertinent relations in terms of the system of which the preposition is a part are different. Thus, if one compares English *in* to French *en*, one can say 'venir *en* auto' but 'to come *by* car', 'être *en* tête' but 'to be *at* the head', 'la suite *en* 4e page' but 'continued *on* page 4', 'professeur *en* Sorbonne' but 'professor *at* the Sorbonne', 'aller *en* Amérique' but 'to go *to* America', etc. Moreover, the fact that in French the present tense is opposed to a past (imperfect) tense as well as a future tense means that the present tense in French is slightly different from the present tense in Russian, because in Russian the whole system of verbal categories is different and especially the role of aspect (1957a). In French, aspect is subordinated to tense and in Russian, tense is subordinated to aspect. In English on the other hand, the simple present (e.g., *kills*) is opposed to a wide range of periphrastic formations referring to present time (e.g., *is killing*, *does kill*, *is being killed*) as well as to simple and periphrastic constructions for the past and the future (1959d). The relational invariance of given items is based upon the relational invariance of the other items in the system.

Another major use of relational invariance in grammar and lexicology parallels that of relational invariance in phonology — the fact that what may seem from the point of view of one language to be quite similar situations may be viewed by another language as quite different, and vice versa. Each classification has its own sense, only it is not a scientific classification. There are simply different principles of division. Thus, for example, in English *bush* and *tree* can refer to two types of vegetation which are actually quite similar, and may be grouped together by other linguistic systems. But the fact of their separation in English is based on a linguistically important difference between them. Similarly, if we take *table* and *chair* in English, there may be certain similarities between *table* and *chair* in their more concrete contextual applications which do not hold between *table* in its concrete use and *table* in its abstract use (*table of random numbers, to table a motion* etc.). But the relevant question is: what is common to all uses of *table* as against all uses of *chair* and does this explain the difference between the concrete use of *table* and the concrete use of *chair* as well as the abstract use of *table* and the abstract use of *chair.*

If we take Jakobson's study of the cases in Russian, the accusative case in Russian is used, among other things, for 'direct objects' of various verbs as well as for 'temporal objects'. Furthermore, the instrumental is used for 'instruments' or 'agents' through which the verbal process is performed as well as for 'temporal objects'. One could say that, from a non-Russian point of view, direct objects and temporal objects are essentially different things, while the temporal objects in the accusative and those in the instrumental are quite similar. Whether this is the right point of view outside of Russian is debatable; but given the fact that meaning systems are not the same, the question is one of equivalence and difference from the point of view of Russian. A closer look at the accusative temporal objects shows that they give, generally, the full temporal expanse of the verbal process, whereas the temporal objects in the instrumental give only a time period within which the verbal process takes place (e.g., *he worked the whole night* = accusative vs. *he worked at night* = instrumental). Coupling these distinctions with that between direct object and agent or instrument, we see that the accusative invariantly gives either a time period or an object which is completely enveloped by the process, while the instrumental invariantly gives either a time period or an object which is an accessory to or peripheral to the process.

Similarly, if we take the preposition *by* in English there seem to be large differences between the use of *by* in, e.g., *he came by Route 79, he was found by the lake, he was killed by a passing car, he was killed by that man, I should be home by 2:15* and indeed some of the uses seem to be closer to the uses of other prepositions than to the other uses of *by* (e.g., *on Route 79, beside or near the lake, before 2:15*). But as Jakobson's analysis of the case system has shown, what may seem to be completely different situations are sometimes classed together by a given linguistic system while what may seem to be quite similar situations can be classed differently. What is common to all the uses of *by* is the following: (1) a relation is set up between the object of the preposition (e.g., *the lake* or *2:15*) and its modified element (e.g., *he was found* or *I should be home*) through the intermediary of the preposition itself; (2) the relation is one in which the object and the modified element are closely linked but still remain separate elements — they do not amalgamate but retain their separate identities (compare, in this respect, *in*: *he was found in the lake* vs. *he was found by the lake*; or *at*: *I should be home at 2:15* vs. *I should be home by 2:15*); (3) the exact nature of the linkage will depend on the verbalized (and/or verbalizable) context in which *by* is used. Thus one gets a locational linkage in *he was found by the lake*, an agentive linkage in *he was killed by that man*, an instrumental linkage in *he was killed by a passing car*, a means linkage in *he came by Route 79*, a temporal linkage in *I should be home by 2:15*.

Another extremely important point about relational invariance discussed in connection with the distinctive features is the notion that a given feature may be interpreted slightly differently depending on the simultaneous environment in which it is used. Thus, for instance, directionality marks both the accusative and the genitive in *-a* in Russian (1958b), but whereas it has the contextual variants of 'goal' or 'complete overlap' in the accusative, it has more the contextual variant of 'focussing' in the genitive. The difference is due to the fact that in the genitive, directionality is in combination with quantification, while in the accusative it is not. A similar example of relational invariance comes from my own study of English. In the prepositional system I have discerned the feature of [+dimensionality] for both *in* and *with*, but there is a slight difference between the two. *In* basically has dimensionality in the sense that the object of the preposition is perceived as having dimensions or limits; the modified element of the preposition is seen as being contained within or interior to those dimensions or limits (e.g., *he is in the house, he is walking in the field*). *With* also posits dimensions or limits, but in this case the dimensions are those of the object and the modified element together (*he sang the opera with me, he talked with friends*). This difference is due to the fact that *with* has another feature which *in* does not have.

Further examples of relational invariance come from the use of given features in various sub-systems. [+marginality] in Russian is the marking for the instrumental, dative, and locatives in the case system, where it basically has the contextual variants of secondariness, peripherality, accessoriness, temporariness, accidentalness. It also marks the preterit in the verbal grammatical system: here, the contextual variant of temporariness comes to the fore and implies cancellation of a previous state or action, non-observability of the state or action, and irreality (this is based on work by C. H. van Schooneveld). The prefix *pere* (van Schooneveld, MS) is also marked by [+marginality]; for *pere* the contextual variants are basically temporariness, peripherality, cancellation. The differences in the contextual variants have to do with the total concurrent context in which marginality is used — nominal meaning vs. verbal meaning vs. prepositional meaning.

Other examples of relational invariance with respect to the concurrent context come from my work on French (Waugh 1976b). The feature of dimensionality marks *en* and *dans* in French (both for the most part implying the same things as *in* in English), *avec* (implying that the object and the modified element together form the dimensions) and *sans* (the cancellation of *avec*), *entre* and *parmi* (implying that the object is some sort of enclosure for the modified element), *entrer* and *sortir* (where the motion ends up in or starts from an enclosure), *maison* and *voiture* (enclosures), the derivational suffix *-ée* (as in *cueillierée*, the contents of a spoon, spoonful; *journée*, a specifically defined part of the more general day, daytime; *pensée* where the fluid nature of thinking is made into a unit, a thought); the pronoun *se* (which confines the verbal process to its subject only); the past participle (in which the verbal process is seen as having a completion); the parts of speech noun and verb (both of which characterize fully — see van Schooneveld 1960). The seeming chasm between the meanings of the various equivalences comes from the fact that we are dealing here with different subsystems of the language and with various concurrent contexts. But the relational invariance is discernable within the variation.

A further, very telling fact with respect to the notion of relational invariance, and one which has been emphasized by Jakobson in agreement with the teaching of Boas and Sapir (1944; 1959d) is that, in general, grammatical meaning is an obligatory category, (the speaker must make a choice between alternatives), whereas lexical meaning isn't. This means, for instance, that if a speaker wants to use a noun in Russian, he must use it in one of the (potentially 8) cases. He must make a choice. And, on the other hand, everything known or to be known must be expressible in one of the 8 cases — the cases must in some way divide the world of human experience into 8 case categories. Given this, it is not surprising that the case meanings are fairly general and subject to wide shifts in variation given the concurrent and sequential context. In French, masculine gender is used for male (animate) beings (e.g., *poulain*), a general designation of an animate class (e.g., *cheval*), a general designation of a human being (e.g., *homme, professeur*), sexless reference (e.g., *mur*), while the feminine gender is used for female (animate) beings (e.g., *femme*), general designations of certain animate classes (e.g., *abeille*), sexless referents (e.g., *chaise*), as well as for certain categories which pertain to both males and females (e.g., *vedette, personne, sentinelle*). The fact that both masculine and feminine nouns may be used for general designation of animate classes as well as for special classes of human beings should not be construed as showing that the gender distinction is meaningless or arbitrary but rather that a simple one-to-one relationship between sex and gender does not exist, although there does seem to be, as Pichon (Damourette et Pichon 1911–30) puts it, '*sexuisemblance*'. Since all nouns in French have to be in one of the two genders, the *principium divisionis* in particular for sexless objects is hard to define and may appear fairly *ad hoc* and abstract at first. However, it does seem to be based on sexual differences or on a metaphorical relationship with sexual differences — and it is true that in figurative usage or in personnification, the principle of sexuisemblance is followed. (Jakobson has also pointed out many examples of this in connection with Russian and German — see 1959a).

Universal Invariance

One of the most important of the ways in which the notion of invariance is realized is UNIVERSAL INVARIANTS of a strictly relational character. These invariants prove once again the non-arbitrary character of language as well as the law-governed nature of language patterning. Furthermore, the full relationship between universals and the ORDER OF ACQUISITION in child language or ORDER OF BREAKUP IN APHASIA and the problems of hierarchy discussed earlier needs exploration. In addition, universals may be divided into those characteristics which are universal to (and thus defining of) language in general, as against those characteristics which are found in almost all languages (NEAR-UNIVERSALS) or in a large number of languages. The latter are equally as important as the former, and indeed the presence of near-universals demands that the exceptions be investigated thoroughly and in relation to the other elements of the system and that the specificity of the explanation of the exceptions be found. And finally, with universals as with everything else, the context-sensitive nature of language is extremely important. This is seen most specifically with '*implicational universals*' — where the 'context' is the total paradigmatic structure of the language.

There are certain 'defining characteristics' (universals) of language which differentiate language from other communication systems:

Several essential properties notably separate verbal signs from all kinds of animal messages: the imaginative and creative power of language; its ability to handle abstractions or fictions and to deal with things and events remote in space and/or time, in contradiction to the hic et nunc of animal signals; that structural hierarchy of linguistic constituents which was labelled 'double articulation' in D. Bubrix's keen essay of 1930 about the uniqueness and origin of human language, namely the dichotomy of merely distinctive (phonemic) and significative (grammatical) units and a further scission of the grammatical pattern into the word and sentences levels (coded units vs. coded matrices); the use of diremes, especially judgmental propositions; and finally, the assemblage and reversible hierarchy of diverse concurrent verbal functions and operations: referential, conative, emotive, phatic, poetic, metalinguistic.... The number of distinct signals produced by an animal is restricted, so that the entire corpus of the different messages is tantamount to their code. (1973e, 44; cf. also 1975d)

And there are also certain universal and near-universal statements (UNIVERSAL TENDENCIES) which one can make concerning the inner structure of the patterning. In addition, Jakobson has said that virtually all languages differentiate phoneme, syllable, word, phrase, clause, sentence, utterance, discourse; and whereas not all languages may have the distinction morpheme vs. word, yet all seem to have the distinction grammatical meaning vs. lexical meaning, whether at the morphological or word level:

'To me the principle of the two different levels: morpheme and word is a universal, although there are languages, like Chinese, with monosyllabic words. These, however, have elaborated the concept of the difference between empty words and full words which corresponds to the difference between grammatical morphemes and lexical morphemes.' (1972b, 31).

But it should be remembered from the outset that invariants are equivalences across languages and that "an interlingual difference in contextual variants does not affect the equivalence of invariant oppositions" (1963a, 588). On the other hand, the invariants themselves must have some foundation in relations, in some kind of formal expression, and in the linguistic sign. Thus, for instance, it is the case that in nearly all languages of the world, in the unmarked word order, the subject precedes the object in the sentence. (This also expresses a near-universal iconic patterning.) Now, the concrete manifestations of this particular phenomenon are quite varied in terms of the actual forms of the words, and their specific position with respect to the verb (e.g., SVO, SOV, VSO); and the rule holds whether or not the subject/object relationship is given in terms of cases or not. In addition, all languages have a distinction noun/verb, even though the exact formal manifestation of the difference, the various functions which nouns and verbs may have in a sentence, and the different contextual variants which nouns and verbs may have differ from language to language. On the other hand, all languages have the distinction subject/predicate — and furthermore the correlation between subject and noun on the one hand and predicate and verb on the other hand is a universal tendency. Furthermore, certain iconic types of patterning are universal — if a language has a singular/plural distinction, then the normal way of making the distinction formally is in terms of a non-zero affix for the plural, thus creating an iconic distinction between 'more quantity' in terms of the meaning and 'more quantity' (or 'more complexity') in terms of the form. Likewise, in those languages which have a case system, the marked cases are normally more complex formally than the unmarked case, although interesting reversals of the normal pattern occur in given languages (e.g., the reversal between zero affix in either the nominative singular or the genitive plural in Russian noun declensions — 1957b — although the zero affix in the genitive plural is rare in terms of the overall inventory). But such reversals always demand an explanation.

On the other hand, it is not so that all languages have a case system — if by case we mean formal distinctions between nouns due to their function in the clause. If by case we mean 'relationships' between various nouns and the verb, then all languages can express such relationships — but they do so in various ways. And the 'ways' in which they are expressed as well as the larger system into which such 'ways' are integrated are important for language TYPOLOGY.

One can, of course, get MARKEDNESS REVERSALS across languages. With respect to case systems, one can compare the markedness of the object in relation to the subject in the nominative/accusative type of language with the opposite distribution in the ergative type of language.

With respect to phonological patterning, CV is the universal (or nearly universal) syllable type — but on the one hand, in various languages it may be opposed to other, and varied, syllable types; and on the other hand, the types of consonants and the types of vowels which can be used vary greatly from language to language. Moreover, all languages have the distinction compact/diffuse in their phonemic system, but the degree of utilization of this opposition differs from one language to another.

But perhaps the most important and most interesting universals are IMPLICATIONAL ones. The question is not only which elements do or do not exist, but also "What elements may occur together and what elements may not? What elements necessarily occur together? Which element A implies which element B, and what elements don't imply each other? Which elements imply the absence of which other element?" (1953c, 563). Many of these universals are at the basis of the hierarchy of distinctive features discussed earlier — they give, in effect, certain structural types and structural laws of patterning. For example, the degree of utilization of nasality for vowels and consonants is completely different. Nasal consonants are nearly universal; nasal vowels are not. Furthermore, within the nasal consonants, if a language has the difference between /ñ/ and /ŋ/, then it will also differentiate /n/ and /m/ — i.e. the differentiation of grave/acute within the compact nasals implies a concomitant differentiation of grave/acute within the diffuse nasals.

The presence of the compact/diffuse opposition in the phonemic system of language implies the presence of the grave/acute opposition. In fact, such implicational statements are at the basis of the problem of TYPOLOGY (thus Jakobson's constant call for a 'phonemic atlas' of the world, which was unfortunately hampered or delayed by diverse obstacles) and of the types and functions of language change (convergence and divergence). The universal laws restrict the number and diversity of structural types and reveal the inner law-governed nature of structural patterning. In addition, Jakobson has discerned not only a 'universal' stock of phonological distinctive features, but also universal tendencies in terms of their HIERARCHY. (See the discussion of markedness to follow.) The problem of the universal stock (existence and implication) of grammatical features and universal tendencies of hierarchy is under discussion. And as Jakobson has said, "The quest for universals is organically linked with all other manifestations of a unitary attitude toward language and linguistics". (1963a, 591) The quest for the typology of given languages, as well as for the universal laws governing the typological patternings, points up again the nomothetic character of linguistics. But here as elsewhere, the principle of relational invariance is important.

MARKEDNESS

Having discussed relational invariance, we may now return to the notion of opposition and a further characterization of opposition: the HIERARCHICAL RELATION between the two poles of an opposition, the unmarked term and the marked term. In general, the marked term of an opposition provides an additional, more specific piece of information (see 1972b) in comparison with the unmarked term. The type of information is, of course, dependent on the particular dimension which underlies the opposition.

In general, there is a PRIORITY of the unmarked term over the marked term. Thus, that which will become the unmarked term in an opposition tends to be learned earlier by children while the marked term tends to be learned later (see 1941; 1949c, 1956a), although of course, their status as unmarked/marked is not established until the marked term is learned. In aphasic loss, the marked term tends to be lost earlier (thus dissolving the opposition) and that which was the unmarked term is lost later (see 1955; 1956b; 1964a; 1966f; 1975e). In phonological oppositions, it is the unmarked term which normally occurs in places of neutralization. On the other hand, it is not necessarily the case that the marked term is less frequent than the unmarked term,[18] for frequency does not have a one-to-one relationship with the notion of markedness: frequency and markedness are relatively autonomous.

Instances where all of this is not the case are rare and do not invalidate the nature of marked/unmarked but demand a supplementary explanation. Thus, for example, Russian children learn the (marked) palatalized dentals before they do the unpalatalized dentals, while the bilabials are unpalatalized (e.g. *p* vs. *t'*). This is, however, due to the fact that one gets an opposition of low tonality (the grave, non-sharp *p*) vs. high tonality (the acute, sharp *t'*), thus creating a clear perceptual distinction between the two pairs of consonants. In French, there is a tendency for the tense vowels to occur in the absolute word final, whereas the lax vowels occur in final syllables closed by a consonant (thus it is sometimes the marked vowels which occur in places of neutralization, sometimes the unmarked vowels). This is probably due to the relation between the length of the vowel and the type of syllable: vowels

[18]This is a point which Greenberg (1966) in particular did not take into account.

are shorter (laxer) in syllables ending with a consonant and longer (tenser) in syllables not ending with a consonant (see 1949d).

Distinctive Features

With respect to distinctive features (i.e. in phonology), the opposition of marked/unmarked is given by PRESENCE/ABSENCE[19] of a certain property (e.g., nasal/non-nasal), although "this absence may be supplemented by the presence of a contrary property" (1962b, 634), e.g. tense/lax. Thus, the presence of nasality ([+nasal]) is a mark or is marked whereas its absence ([−nasal]) is unmarked, is not a mark. Markedness in phonology is based on the distinctive function of the features and of their combinations. In addition, markedness is contextually defined, for it depends on the CONCURRENT CONTEXT in which a given feature will occur; in studying the distribution of marked and unmarked terms, one must take into account the contextual relations of the given opposition with the surrounding oppositions. For example, stridency (vs. mellowness) is marked in concurrent combination with abruptness but unmarked in connection with continuousness in the obstruents. Furthermore, consonants as a class are unmarked as against vowels. In fact, consonant/vowel is the basic opposition of all phonological systems, and the one upon which most other markedness values are based. Thus, for instance, in the vowels, compactness (e.g., /a/) is unmarked, whereas in the consonants diffuseness (e.g., /p/ and /t/) is unmarked, giving the basic opposition *p-t-a*. In the vowels, the diffuse vowels /i/ and /u/ (marked for being non-compact) supplement the unmarked compact /a/, while in the consonants the marked /k/ supplements the /p/ and /t/, thus giving the famous triple phonological triangles (1956a, 40):

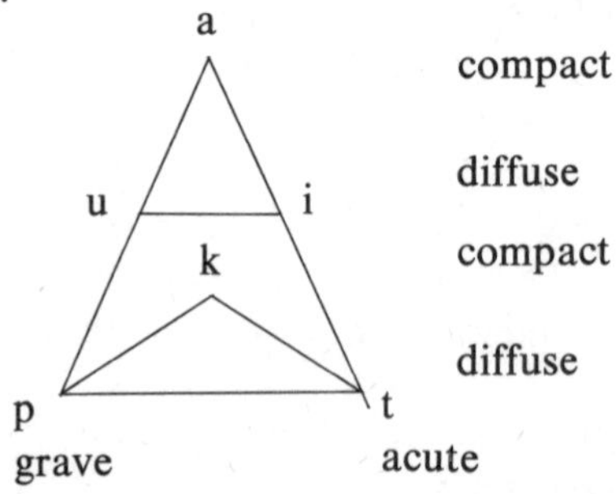

[19]This absence has been called a 'zero property' or 'zero quality' by Jakobson (1939b; 1940).

where the apex of the triangle is unmarked in the vowels and marked in the consonants.

If we return to nasality now, in phonemic systems of languages of the world, the tendency to have nasal consonants is near-universal, whereas nasal vowels are rare. This is due to the fact that consonants are unmarked and vowels are marked, and to the fact that there is a TENDENCY NOT TO ACCUMULATE MARKS. Since nasality is a mark, it tends to be used with the unmarked consonants more than with the marked vowels. In child language acquisition, nasal consonants are acquired before nasal vowels and bring the first combination of an open and a closed resonator (see 1941; 1956a); nasal consonants always appear before nasal vowels in child language acquisition and disappear after nasal vowels in aphasic loss; in languages of the world, the presence of nasal vowels in a language implies the presence of nasal consonants but not *vice versa* (see 1963a).

The tendency for the non-accumulation of marks (for the superposition of markedness on unmarkedness) is particularly evident in certain usual SYNCRETISMS of features. In vowels, the habitual syncretism of marks gives gravity with flatness and acuteness with non-flatness (i.e. back rounded vowels vs. front unrounded vowels). In the consonants, the usual syncretism is for tenseness with voicelessness (e.g. /t/) and laxness with voicing (e.g. /d/) on the one hand, and stridency with continuousness (e.g. /s/) and mellowness with non-continuousness (e.g. /t/) on the other hand. If such a syncretism is split into three terms, then the tendency is for the non-combination of two marks (i.e. a normal 3-way system would give *t*-t^h-*d*, and only rarely is the doubly marked d^h found). Such syncretisms are basic for a large number of phonological systems, and SCISSION of the syncretisms is SECONDARY.[20] In such syncretisms, the question of which feature is distinctive and which is redundant depends on the particular linguistic system—i.e. in Japanese grave/acute is the distinctive opposition while flat/plain is the redundant one; in Russian it is the other way around. Evidence for the differentiation of distinctive vs. redundant comes from places of assimilation, places of neutralization, the type and variety of contextual variants, etc. as well as, for example, mistakes which speakers of one language make in learning another language. Thus, the front rounded vowel /ø/ in the French word *jeu* was, according to Jakobson (1952, 10),

[20]The secondary character of the scissions is evident in a synchronic sense, in terms of typological patterning and of universal tendencies to avoid scissions and in a diachronic sense, in terms of the prior temporal existence of the syncretism before the scission takes place.

rendered by [o] by a Russian and by [e] by a Slovak, thus showing that for the Russian the flatness was decisive whereas for the Slovak the acuteness was decisive. It is, of course, true, that in some cases of very strong syncretism, there may be no possibility of differentiating the distinctive vs. the redundant features: it is the combination of the features which functions distinctively.

The opposition of a one-feature glide with a ZERO PHONEME is one of the more controversial of Jakobson's applications of the notion of opposition, of markedness, and of the 'zero sign' in phonology. For Jakobson, a glide is basically a one-feature phoneme opposed to a zero and moreover is normally found in only one position or at least in a limited number of positions in the word. If we take the glide in English (1952, 43) it is tense and in the word initial and before a vowel, the opposition is implemented as /h/ vs. the zero phoneme, glottal catch (*hit* vs *it*); in rapid speech in the phrase-medial the glottal catch may not be realized, may be a true zero. In French, where the one-feature glide is also tense (1977), the opposition is implemented as the potentiality of a realization (either as [e] or as 'h aspiré') vs. no potentiality of a realization (a true zero). In Russian, where the one-feature glide is sharp, the opposition is implemented as yod vs. no yod. The category of zero phoneme is, then, strictly tied to the notion of opposition, and not at all liable to be posited at will and uncontrollably.

Conceptual Features

The markedness relation for conceptual features is slightly different from that of distinctive features. In the signatum, marked [+feature A] means the necessary presence of the information given by the feature in all the contexts, in all the uses of the particular item. In other words, the item invariantly carries whatever unit of information is given by the feature. Unmarked [∅ feature A] means that the information given by feature A is not necessarily present in all the contexts in which the unmarked form occurs. It means either presence or absence of that particular piece of information. The item remains neutral, uncommitted with regard to the information given by A.[21] Thus the opposition is one of a DETERMINATE term vs. an INDETERMINATE term.

[21] Thus, Jakobson calls unmarked the 'zero meaning' (*Nullbedeutung, signification zéro*) (1939b; 1940). The recognition of a 'zero property' for the unmarked term in phonology and 'zero meaning' for the unmarked term in grammar/lexicology unites the sense of unmarked in the two systems.

Examples of marked/unmarked relationships in grammar and lexicology include the following: (1) in the case system of Russian, accusative [+directionality] vs. nominative [∅ directionality], dative [+marginality, +directionality] vs. instrumental [+marginality, ∅directionality] and so forth (1936; 1958b); (2) in Russian, the plural [+more than one] vs. singular [∅ more than one] (1932a; 1957b); (3) in Russian, the perfective aspect [+absolute completion of the verbal process] vs. imperfective aspect [∅absolute completion] (1957a); (4) in English, *woman* [+female] vs. *man* [∅female]; (5) English *mare* [+female] and *stallion* [+male] vs. *horse* [∅female, ∅male]; (6) English *out* [+dimensionality, +cancellation] vs. *in* [+dimensionality, ∅cancellation] (see also van Schooneveld MS[22]); (7) in Russian, animate [+animateness] vs. inanimate [∅animateness] (1957a); (8) in the wide-spread system of the so-called 'personal' pronouns (discussed earlier), the first and second person [+participants of the speech event] vs. 3rd [∅participants of the speech event]; 1st person [+producer of the given message] vs. 2nd person [∅producer of the given message] (1957a); (9) the passive voice or a passive construction is marked as against the active by a "shift in semantic perspective from the agent to the goal . . . and allowing the omission of the agent" (1972a); (10) predicative use of the adjective vs. attributive use is marked by a greater autonomy of the adjective in predication from the noun which it modifies (1941); (11) in French, the word order adjective-noun is marked by a deictic anticipation of the lexical meaning of the adjective while the order noun-adjective is unmarked (Waugh 1976a; 1977); (12) in Russian, the non-use of the personal pronoun subject is stylistically marked while the use of the personal pronoun subject is unmarked; in Czech, the use of the personal pronoun subject is expressively marked while its non-use is unmarked. (This is akin to the so-called 'zero of expressivity' noted for the presence of the copula in Latin vs. its absence.) (1939b; 1940)

It should be clear from the above that to say that two terms are in a marked/unmarked opposition is to say that each is marked or unmarked for a given feature, with respect to a particular unit of information. It is not a characterization of the term as a whole. In fact the two terms will have other markings in addition. (No term in language is

[22] If we take an example like *out*, we can see why it would be a mistake to define it as [−dimensionality] (the absence of dimensionality) for *out* in many cases presupposes a previous *in* situation which is cancelled and cancellation of an *in* situation is very different from [−dimensionality], which would deny the relevance of dimensions for the given situation.

completely unmarked — all terms convey some conceptual information.) Secondly, it is not the case that all signs, even of a small grammatical system, are in a simple marked/unmarked relationship — the instrumental and the genitive in Russian are differentiated by the fact that the instrumental is marked for [+marginality] while the genitive is unmarked for it, and the genitive is marked for [+quantification] while the instrumental is unmarked for it. On the other hand, the dative and the locative share a marking ([+directionality]) but in addition the dative is marked for [+directionality] and the locative is marked for [+quantification] (1936; 1958b). And so on.

Gesamtbedeutung, Grundbedeutung

The indeterminate nature of the unmarked term leads to another extremely important factor of the opposition marked/unmarked. If we take the information given by the marked term, then there is an INCLUSION RELATION, a set (unmarked term) vs. a subset (marked term) relationship between them (a classic case of a part/whole relationship):[23]

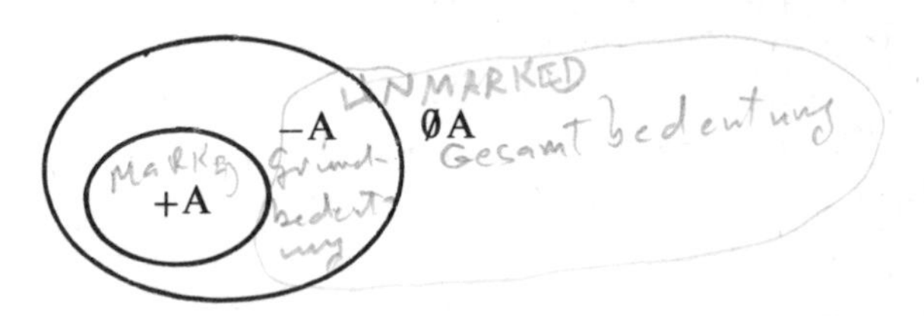

where the sets do not refer to ranges of contextual variation, distribution, type of usage, etc. but rather to the unit of information conveyed. If we take [+directionality] = accusative as against [Ødirectionality] = nominative, then the accusative necessarily always conveys the information given by [+directionality] while the nominative by itself says nothing in this respect.

Jakobson has emphasized the importance of the difference for the unmarked term between the non-signalization of A = [ØA] (the *Gesamtbedeutung* or 'general meaning' of the category) and the signalization of non-A = [−A] (the *Grundbedeutung* or 'basic' meaning of the category) (1932a; 1936). The signalization of non-A is the chief but not the ex-

[23] This diagram is from C. H. van Schooneveld (MS).

clusive use of the unmarked term and furthermore "on the level of general meaning the opposition of the two contradictories may be interpreted as 'statements of A' vs. 'no statement of A', whereas on the level of 'narrowed', nuclear meanings, we encounter the opposition 'statement of A' vs. 'statement of non-A'". (1957a, 136).

Several things should be clear from this difference. First of all, the *Gesamtbedeutung* gives to the unmarked term the potentiality of being VAGUE (or ambiguous) *vis-à-vis* the information given by the marked term. If the speaker uses *at* and not *in* for the sentence *they are at the house*, *at* potentially can include situations where the persons involved are inside or outside the house (or both). But it can also be the case that the speaker simply doesn't know whether *they* are inside or outside; or the speaker may be deliberately non-committal; or the speaker may not care; or their position *vis-à-vis* the inside of the house may be irrelevant; or etc. All of these are possible and are built into the notion of *Gesamtbedeutung*. A close look at this aspect of the marked/unmarked relationship, at the differentiation of general and contextual meanings, and at the generic meaning of any sign whatsoever, shows that what in many cases are at first glance 'ambiguous' constructions are really only the products of the vagueness (or generic character) of linguistic meaning and the lack of certain markings. For instance, if we take the preposition *of* and the phrases *the shooting of the hunters* and the corresponding sentences *the hunters are shooting* and *X is shooting the hunters*, the more precise specification of the latter two sentences *vis-à-vis* the nominalization shows that *of* is vague with respect to the difference subject/object. It gives a relationship between *the hunters* and *the shooting* without specifying more precisely the subject or object nature of the relationship. Moreover, the *Gesamtbedeutung* permits such phrases as *the short stick is 11 inches long; the first representative of Cro-Magnon man found was a woman; he goes to work every day, but today he stayed home*, etc. (See Holenstein, 1974, for similar examples.)

Furthermore, the concept of *Gesamtbedeutung* means that something can be seen as two things at once. Prepositional phrases are both adjectival and adverbial, depending on whether they modify a noun or a verb; and in certain contextual uses they may still be vague and interpreted as either one or the other or both: *I wrote the book at that table*. The attributive vs. predicative function is due to the unmarked nature of the preposition in terms of type of modification.

Secondly, many items will have two major meanings—one conveyed by the *Gesamtbedeutung* and one conveyed by the *Grundbedeutung*. Thus, as Jakobson has pointed out (1932a, 4), Russian *osël* is the word both for the species *ass* in its *Gesamtbedeutung* and for *jackass* in its *Grundbedeutung*. On the other hand, its marked opposite *oslica* can be used only for the *she-ass*. Similarly, the *Gesamtbedeutung* of the nominative case is the pure naming function: e.g. names of stores, dictionary listing, whereas its *Grundbedeutung* is its use for the subject of the predication (1936). The *Gesamtbedeutung* of the present tense in many languages is the lack of any specification of time (*man is an animal*) whereas its *Grundbedeutung* is the reference to present time = simultaneity with the speech event (*Spring begins today*). The differentiation of *Grundbedeutung* as against *Gesamtbedeutung* may also be a clue as to how to approach the enormous problem of syntax and how to understand why certain lexical items in combination with certain others force the interpretation in a given direction. In contexts where the unmarked and marked terms are both used, and are differentiated, the unmarked term takes on the *Grundbedeutung* interpretation: *a man and a woman*; *did a man come?, no, a woman did.*

In certain specialized instances, the unmarked term may be used for the signalization of A (called 'a not proper use'[24] in 1936; 1958b): e.g., the 'historical present', the use of the present for the future, the nominative in a passive sentence used for the goal of the action. Such use is not illegitimate, but may leave in doubt the particular interpretation intended because of the potential capacity of the unmarked term for the more generalized interpretation. The intended interpretation may be dependent on the context for disambiguation.

A further example of the hierarchical arrangement of contextual variants comes from the figurative use of signs (metaphor and metonymy). Such figurative uses are completely normal — there is transfer between non-figurative and figurative meanings the whole time. If metaphors constitute an imputed similarity (i.e. the axis of selection) between the normal referents of a given sign and other referents, this raises serious questions not only for the relationship between the basic and contextually given meanings of particular signs, but also for the relation between the invariant and the variants. The separation of the invariant from its contextual meanings assures the fact that metaphors are not deviant, but rather are certain expressively marked uses of given signs; this separation also means that metaphors are a viable and completely

[24] Also known as hypostasis.

normal part of language use and do not invalidate the relational invariant associated with any given sign. Just as in phonology we cannot treat all sounds as being equal in terms of 'expressive' or 'stylistic' value, so in lexicology the variants are not only hierarchized but also expressively and stylistically different. To treat *you're a chicken* on a par with other uses of *chicken* is to forget the difference between the various uses in terms of their relation to the place of the word *chicken* in the structure of language. On the other hand, *you're a chicken* is a codified expression, codified as 'similar to a chicken in certain respects which are culturally given', whereas *you're a penguin* is not codified. In the latter, the question may legitimately be asked: 'in what way are you using penguin?'.

In certain contexts, the unmarked term may seem to give additional information not connected with the marking and this information is not provided by the marked term. Thus, to take the examples *at* vs. *in*, the sentences *she is at the office* and *she is in the office* both may be used for situations in which *she* is actually within the confines of the *office*. But the use of *at* in such a sentence further implies that the office is her normal place of work, whereas *in* may imply just the opposite. This is due to the fact that *in* focusses on the dimensions given by the office, while *at* doesn't. Thus, *in* may imply that the dimensions are relevant for a particular reason — i.e., that the office is not a usual place to be; given this, *at* then is interpreted as the normal place for her to be (and thus the place where she works).[25]

The tendency towards SYNCRETISMS and toward the NON-ACCUMULATION OF MARKS noted for distinctive features is also prevalent for conceptual features. In Russian, the singular of adjectives differentiates three genders in the nominative and two in the other cases, while the plural differentiates none. In the present tense in Russian, three persons and two numbers are distinguished, while in the preterit only the two numbers remain, with a concomitant distinction of three genders in the unmarked singular number. The pronouns exhibit the same distinction of three genders in the unmarked third personal singular. Furthermore, there are IMPLICATIONS evident for grammar — e.g., no language has a dual without having also a plural and a singular. Moreover, markedness relations may depend on the CONCURRENT contexts in certain cases —

[25]I would like to thank Dwight L. Bolinger for his stimulating comment on an earlier version of this work which led to this discussion.

e.g., Jakobson's discussion of the neuter as marked for [+non-reference to an animate being] in the noun as against its being unmarked ([Øsubject expressed]) in the preterit (1960c). And MARKEDNESS ASSIMILATION (the interaction of the markings of given items in larger syntactic matrices) may well account for the interpretation particular combinations may receive.

An example of the REVERSABILITY OF MARKING due to the sequential context is inspired by certain comments of Elmar Holenstein (Holenstein 1974, 159–160) on the reversability of marked/unmarked in lexical items. The two adjectives *near* and *far* in English in terms of their invariant are in a marked (*near*) vs. unmarked (*far*) relationship. And, when used in a context where no presuppositions as to closeness being the normal relationship are present, the markings hold: *the train station is just as far from the center of town as is the bus station* (where it is not said what the distance is) vs. *the train station is just as near to the center of town as is the bus station* (where the expectation is that they are both close to the center of town). However, in a context where nearness, a close relationship, is expected, then the use of *far* becomes marked (*I feel myself just as near to my sister as to my brother* vs. *I feel myself just as far from my sister as from my brother* — in the latter case it is said that the speaker is indeed far from both, whereas in the former case the actual distance is not known). But the reversal is given only because of the presence of a norm which forces the interpretation in a given direction.

Parallel between Phonology and Grammar/Lexicology

There is then a striking parallel between the phonological system and the grammatical and lexicological system of language. We have seen that for Jakobson the phonological system of language is made up of 'ultimate constituents' — a small set of BINARY PHONOLOGICAL FEATURES, either inherent or prosodic — in a distinctive function. Furthermore, they combine in various ways to form larger wholes — the phonemes — of given languages. Moreover, the inherent features have a HIERARCHICAL arrangement defineable through the structural laws of the system. In the grammatical (and lexicological) system there seems to be a set of BINARY FEATURES in a conceptual function, which define, through binary oppositions and in various combinations, the larger wholes — the morphemes and words — of the given language. Furthermore, the conceptual features may well have a HIERARCHICAL arrangement through their conceptual, inherent nature.[26] Thus, not only is the close connection between signans and signatum in the linguistic sign confirmed, but also the relative autonomy of the two in addition to their integration in terms of similarities of patterning.

On the other hand, there is an essential difference between the signans and the signatum in the sense that the former are PERCEPTS, perceptual categories actually residing in the speech sounds, whereas the latter are CONCEPTS, conceptual categories which organize the semiotic system of the world of human experience. The latter are not percepts in the sense that they are directly perceivable neither in the sounds nor in ontological reality — they by themselves are 'conveyable' or 'intelligible' or 'translatable', but not perceivable.[27]

The separation of meaning from reference, the vague and generic character of meaning and of the narrated event, the strictly linguistic character of meaning, the close relation of meaning and form in the linguistic sign, the opposition of marked and unmarked, the notion of the distinctive feature, the notion of relational invariance, the relationship of deixis to the distinctive feature, the importance of the speaker/addressee relation, the potentially fictional character of meaning, the closely controlled search for universals and typological laws of patterning, the hierarchical relationship of the features and of the various types of deixis, the relation of meaning to perception—all give a non-arbitrary, empirical, principled basis for doing a linguistic (i.e. structural) study of meaning. On the other hand, a fully linguistic (i.e. significative) study of syntax implies everything which has been said above for meaning, plus the additional problem of the syntactic matrices (and the rules of combination, particularly with respect to general and contextual meanings of words), the relation between the code and the verbalized or verbal-

[26]There also seems to be, according to work done by van Schooneveld (see MS), an intrinsic hierarchy of the conceptual features reflecting in general an unmarked/marked (inclusion) relationship between the features. Furthermore, van Schooneveld has postulated that deixis, rather than being a category or a feature, is actually part of the intrinsic nature of given features, providing a further hierarchical arrangement, with the deictic ones more marked and the non-deictic ones less marked.

[27]Given this we can see why van Schooneveld (MS) has defined linguistic meaning as "cues in force between speaker and addressee for the perception of extra-linguistic reality" where by 'cues' he means essentially the 'intelligible' nature of the signatum and by 'perception of extra-linguistic reality' he means essentially the classification which language provides and which may presuppose patternings which create parts of extra-linguistic reality. Similarly, it shows the importance of the speaker/addressee relationship for meaning. The relationship between meaning and the viewpoint of the observer (see Holenstein 1974 also in this regard) is an important problem.

izable context, the hierarchical relationship of sentence and word, the relatively higher freedom at the syntactic level than at the word level, the hierarchical structure implicit in syntactic patterns (and especially their relationship, on the one hand, to attribution and predication and on the other hand, to such language-specific notions as government and agreement), the interrelation of the matrix and the codified words (particularly with respect to the differentiation of lexical meaning and grammatical meaning on the one hand, and of the basic meaning and peripheral meanings on the other), the importance of redundancy, the difference between two levels of grammatical meaning (morphologic and syntactic meaning) and of lexical meaning (vocabulary and phraseology), the highly deictic and context-sensitive nature of syntax, the relationship between selection and combination, the hierarchy of the conceptual features and the relative hierarchy given by the marked/unmarked relationships.

CONCLUSION

In summary, then, there are certain 'cardinal' principles of linguistic organization which underlie and integrate Jakobson's science of language — in particular, the RELATIVE AUTONOMY of language itself as well as of all of its parts; the TELEOLOGICAL FOUNDATION of language and of all of its parts and the means-ends relationship between CODE and MESSAGE; indissoluble ties between the STATIC and DYNAMIC aspects of language; the opposition between SELECTION and COMBINATION as two relatively autonomous axes upon which given items operate; the LINGUISTIC SIGN, implying the intimate connection between the signans and the signatum and the strictly linguistic, discrete nature of both sound and meaning; the logical structure of binary OPPOSITIONS in a hierarchized and mutually implicating relationship; the RELATIONAL INVARIANCE of any facet of language from the largest to the smallest, each one built on the strictly relational nature of language; and MARKEDNESS, and in particular the unequal hierarchical relation between the marked and unmarked members of any opposition. All of these are interrelated and depend upon the others for their existence in the system. For, of course, these general principles of organization are systematic both in the sense that they permeate all levels and all facets of language, and in the sense that they are intertwined and can be understood only in terms of one another.

But perhaps the greatest teaching of Jakobson has been not only in terms of language structure, but also in WAYS OF THINKING: in terms of RELATIVITY, not absoluteness; in terms of RELATIONS, not things; in terms of FUNCTION, not thingness; in terms of HIERARCHY, not equality; in terms of the correlation between INVARIANTS and variation; in terms of LAW-GOVERNED patterning, deprived of arbitrariness; in terms of EQUIVALENCE IN DIFFERENCE, and not mechanical resemblances and differences; in terms of SYSTEMS, not atomized units; in terms of STRUCTURE, not agglomeration.

And what emerges from Jakobson's work is not only a consistently integrated and highly original view of language; there is also a profound belief in language and, in addition, an abiding belief that the principles just discussed have proven to be, and will prove to be, those which are in fact intrinsic to language structure. Jakobson's work in the past, and his continuous research has always been and still is based on the fact that these principles (and any new ones which might be discovered) underlie and define the essence of language, and that any work in linguistics proper, as well as in the relationship between language and various other structures, as for instance society, the brain, cognition, music, genetics, must take into account the insights we already have. In fact, Jakobson has himself stated (in lectures and discussion) that if he were a young scholar starting out now he would study systematically the language of schizophrenia, because that is an area where one can get essential new insights both into the structural variety of language and into the diagnosis of schizophrenic disorders, as he shows in his newest observations of the language and poetry of Hölderlin after forty years of the poet's acute mental illness (1976). In reading Jakobson's work from its very beginnings sixty years ago until the present moment, as Whitman says, "a literary imagination such as Jakobson's could hold on to its intuition of the space within language itself until an adequate means for dealing with that space became available" (Whitman 1973, 682), and there is every reason to suppose that in the future work of Jakobson himself and of those linguists who follow in his footsteps, and develop his fundamental ideas, a consistent and rigorous adherence to those principles will lead to the further spectacular progress which linguistics is revealing through the twentieth century.

BIBLIOGRAPHY

BIBLIOGRAPHY OF ROMAN JAKOBSON

1928a The concept of the sound law and the teleological criterion — SWI, 1–2.

1928 Proposition au premier congrès international de linguistes: Quelles sont les méthodes les mieux appropriées à un exposé complet et pratique de la phonologie d'une langage quelconque? (countersigned by S. Karcevski and N. Trubetzkoy) — SWI, 3–6.

1928c Les problèmes des études littèraires et linguistiques — in Todorov, ed., Théorie de la littérature — 138–40 (with J. Tynianov).

1931 Discussion — Réunion phonologique internationale tenue à Prague (18–21/XII 1930) — TCLP IV, 297.

1932a Zur struktur des russischen Verbums — SWII, 3–15.

1932b Musicologie et linguistique — Questions de poétique, 102–4.

1933–4 Co je poesie? = Qu'est-ce que la poésie? — Questions de poétique, 113–26.

1936 Beitrag zur allgemeinen Kasuslehre, Gesamtbedeutungen der russischen Kasus — SWII, 211–19.

1939a Observations sur le classement phonologiques des consonnes — SWI, 272–79.

1939b Signe zéro — SWII, 211–10.

1939c Nikolaj Sergeevič Trubetzkoy (16 avril 1890 — 5 juin 1938) — Essais de linguistique II, 296–311.

1939d Un manuel de phonologie générale — SWI, 311–16.

1939e Zur Struktur des Phonems — SWI, 280–310.

1940 Das Nullzeichen — SWII, 220–22.

1941 Kindersprache, Aphasie und allgemeine Lautgesetze — SWI, 328–401; reference is made to the translation: Child Language, Aphasia and Phonological Universals — The Hague: Mouton (1968).

1942 Six leçons sur le son et le sens — Paris: Editions de Minuit — published 1976 — Préface by Claude Lévi-Strauss.

1943 Polish-Russian cooperation in the science of language — SWII, 451–55.

1944 Franz Boas' approach to language — SWII, 477–88.

1948 Russian conjugation — SWII, 119–29.

1949a Principes de phonologie historique — SWI, 202–20.

1949b Sur la théorie des affinités phonologiques entre les langues — SWI, 234–46.

1949c Les lois phoniques du langage enfantin et leur place dans la phonologie générale — SWI, 317–327.

1949d Notes on the French phonemic pattern — SWI, 426–434 (with John Lotz).

1949e The phonemic and grammatical aspects of language in their interrelations — SWII, 103–14.

1949f On the identification of phonemic entities — SWI, 418–25.

1949g Notes on general linguistics: Its present state and crucial problems — N.Y.: Rockefeller Foundation, Mimeo.
1951 For the correct presentation of phonemic problems — SWI, 435–42.
1952 Preliminaries to speech analysis (the distinctive features and their correlates) — MIT Press (reference is made to the 1961 reprinting) (with Gunnar Fant and Morris Halle).
1953a Toward the logical description of languages in their phonemic aspect — SWI, 449–63.
1953b Patterns in linguistics (contribution to debates with anthropologists) — SWII, 223–28.
1953c Results of a joint conference of anthropologists and linguists — SWII, 554–67.
1955 Aphasia as a linguistic topic — SWII, 229–38.
1956a Fundamentals of language — The Hague: Mouton — (revised edition 1971) — (with Morris Halle)
1956b Two aspects of language and two types of aphasic disturbances — SWII, 239–59.
1956c Metalanguage as a linguistic problem — (Presidential address to the LSA) — in The Scientific Study of Language: Fifty Years of the LSA, 1924–73, ed. by Anwar S. Dil — Abbottabad, Pakistan: Linguistic Research Group of Pakistan — In press.
1956d Serge Karcevski — SWII, 517–21.
1957a Shifters, verbal categories and the Russian verb — SWII, 130–47.
1957b The relationship between genitive and plural in the declension of Russian nouns — SWII, 148–53.
1957c Mufaxxama: The 'emphatic' phonemes in Arabic — SWI, 510–22.
1957d Notes on Gilyak — SWII, 72–97.
1957e The cardinal dichotomy of language — in Language: An enquiry into its meaning and function, ed. by R. Anschen — Science of Culture Series — N.Y.: Harper.
1958a Typological studies and their contribution to historical comparative linguistics — SWI, 523–32.
1958b Morfologičeskie nabljudenija nad slavjanskim skloneniem (Sostav russkix padežnyx form) — SWII, 154–83 (English summary 197–81).
1959a On linguistic aspects of translation — SWII, 260–66.
1959b Note on the tonality features of Roumanian consonantal phonemes — SWI, 661–63.
1959c Linguistic glosses to Goldstein's 'Wortbegriff' — SWII, 267–71.
1959d Boas' view of grammatical meaning — SWII, 489–96.
1959e Trois conférences données à Bucarest les 3 et 6 oct. 1958: Les problèmes les plus actuels de l'étude des sons du langage; Discussion sur la linguistique mathématique; Sur les méthodes d'analyse de la langue — Ms.
1959f Introductory Note — Description and Analysis of Contemporary Standard Russian I — The Hague: Mouton — 5–6 (with C. H. van Schooneveld).
1960a Linguistics and Poetics — in Style in Language, ed. by T. A. Sebeok — Cambridge: MIT Press — 350–77.
1960b Why 'mama' and 'papa'? — SWI, 538–45.
1960c The gender pattern of Russian — SWII, 184–86.
1960d The Kazan school of Polish linguistics and its place in the international development of phonology — SWII, 394–428.
1961a Introduction to the symposium on the structure of language and its mathematical aspects — SWII, 568–69.
1961b Linguistics and communication theory — SWII, 570–79.
1962a On the Rumanian neuter — SWII, 187–89.
1962b Retrospect — SWI, 631–58.

1962c Parts and wholes in language — SWII, 280–84.
1962d Anthony's contribution to linguistic theory — SWII, 285–88.
1962e The phonemic concept of distinctive features (with discussion) — Proceedings of the 4th International Congress of Phonetic Sciences — The Hague: Mouton — 440–55.
1962f Zeichen und System der Sprache — SWII, 272–79.
1963a Implications of language universals for linguistics — SWII, 580–92.
1963b Essais de linguistique générale (I), (Les fondements du langage) — Paris: Editions de Minuit.
1963c Efforts towards a means-ends model of language in interwar continental linguistics — SWII, 522–26.
1964a Toward a linguistic classification of aphasic impairments — SWII, 289–306.
1964b Tenseness and laxness — SWI, 550–55.
1964c Results of the Ninth International Congress of Linguists — SWII, 593–604.
1964d Visual and auditory signs — SWII, 334–37.
1964e Language in operation — Mélanges Alexandre Koyré, I: l'aventure de l'esprit — Paris — 269–81.
1965a An example of migratory terms and institutional models — SWII, 527–30.
1965b Stroj ukrainskogo imperativa — SWII, 190–97.
1966a Quest for the essence of language — SWII, 345–59.
1966b Selected Writings IV, Slavic Epic Studies — The Hague: Mouton — (abbreviated: SWIV).
1966c Retrospect — SWIV, 637–704.
1966d Henry Sweet's path toward phonemics — SWII, 456–67.
1966e Grammatical parallelism and its Russian facet — Language XLII, 399–429.
1966f Linguistic types of aphasia — SWII, 307–33.
1966g Russian stem suffixes and verbal aspects — SWII, 198–202.
1967a On the relation between visual and auditory signs — SWII, 338–44.
1967b Questionner Jakobson — Jean Pierre Faye, Le récit hunique — Paris — 273–85.
1968a The role of phonic elements in speech perception — SWI, 705–19.
1968b Poetry of grammar and grammar of poetry — Lingua 21, 597–609.
1968c Language in relation to other communication systems — SWII, 697–708
1969 Extrapulmonic consonants: Ejectives, implosives, clicks — SWI, 720–27.
1970 Subliminal verbal patterning in poetry — Studies in general and oriental linguistics presented to Shirô Hattori — Tokyo: TEC Co., Ltd. — 302–08.
1971a Selected Writings I, Phonological studies — 2nd, expanded edition — The Hague: Mouton — (abbreviated SWI) — (first edition: 1962).
1971b Selected Writings II, Word and Language—The Hague: Mouton—(abbreviated SWII).
1971c Acknowledgements and dedication — SWII, V–VIII.
1971d Retrospect — SWII, 711–22.
1971e La première lettre de Ferdinand de Saussure à Antoine Meillet sur les anagrammes — Questions de poétique, 190–201.
1971f Krugovorot lingvističeskix terminov — SWI, 734–37.
1971g Saussure's unpublished reflections on phonemes — SWI, 743–52.
1971h The World response to Whitney's principles of linguistic science — in Whitney on Language, ed. by M. Silverstein — Cambridge: MIT Press.
1971i Fundamentals of language — 2nd revised edition — The Hague: Mouton.
1971j Roman Jakobson: A bibliography of his writings — with a foreword by C. H. van Schooneveld — The Hague: Mouton.
1972a Verbal communication — Scientific American, 227, 72–80.
1972b Louvain lectures — ed, by M. van Ballaer as Aspects of the theories of Roman Jakobson — Memoir, Katholieke Universiteit te Leuven.

1972c Entretien de Roman Jakobson avec Jean-Pierre Faye, Jean Paris, et Jacques Roubaud — Hypothèses: Trois entretiens et trois études sur la linguistique et la poétique — Paris: Seghers/Laffont — 33–50.
1972d Entretien sur la mode et la théorie du language — Change 13, 155–63.
1972e The Editor Interviews Roman Jakobson — Modern Occasions 2/1, 14–20.
1973a Questions de poétique — Paris: Editions du Seuil.
1973b Postscriptum — Questions de poétique — 485–504.
1973c Essais de linguistique générale II (Rapports internes et externes du langage) — Paris: Editions de Minuit.
1973d Le concept linguistique des traits distinctifs: réminiscences et méditations — Essais de linguistique générale II,.131–66 (a combination of 1962b and 1962e).
1973e Main trends in the science of language — New York: Harper.
1974a Life and Language — Review of F. Jacob, The Logic of life: A history of heredity — Linguistics, 97–103.
1974b Mark and Feature — Festschrift Kiju, World Papers in Phonetics — Phonetic Society of Japan — 37–39.
1974c Spatial relationships in Slavic adjectives — Scritti in onore di Giuliano Bonfante — Brescia: Paideia Editore — 211–15.
1974d Nachwort to Roman Jakobson, Form und Sinn — München:Fink — 176–77.
1975a Coup d'oeil sur le développement de la sémiotique — Studies in Semiotics — Bloomington: Indiana University Research Center in Language and Semiotic Sciences.
1975b Glosses on the medieval insight into the science of language — Mélanges linguistiques offerts à Emile Benveniste — Paris: Société linguistique de Paris — 289–303.
1975c Structuralisme et téléologie — L'Arc 60, 50–54.
1975d Sur la spécificité du langage humain — L'Arc 60, 3–8.
1975e Les règles des dégâts grammaticaux — in Langue, Discours, Société: Pour Emile Benveniste — sous la direction de Julie Kristeva, Jean-Claude Milner, Nicolas Ruwet — Paris: Seuil — 11–25.
1975f Three linguistic abstracts (I. The Problem of meaning in modern linguistics; II. Diverse aspects of comparative analysis in linguistics; III. Postscript to Main trends in the science of language) — Studii şi cercetari lingvistice dedicated to A. Rosetti — 505–07.
1975g N. S. Trubetzkoy's Letters and Notes — The Hague: Mouton — (with the assistance of H. Baran, O. Ronen, and Martha Taylor) — Foreword, V–XIV.
1976 Hölderlin, Klee, Brecht — Frankfurt-an-Main: Suhrkamp.
1978 The sound shape of language — Bloomington: Indiana University Press — (with Linda R. Waugh).

GENERAL BIBLIOGRAPHY

Bally, Charles 1965 Linguistique générale et linguistique française — 4th edition — Berne: Francke.
Beccaria, Gian Luigi 1968 Origini e caratteri dello strutturalismo — Sigma 18, Guigno, 3–24.
Bell, E. T. 1945 The Development of Mathematics — 2nd editon — New York–London.
Benveniste, Emile 1939 Nature du signe linguistique — in Problèmes de linguistique générale — Paris: Gallimard (1966) — 49–55.
—— 1962 'Structure' en linguistique — in Sens et usages du terme Structure (2nd edition, 1972), ed. by Roger Bastide — The Hague: Mouton — 31–39.

Bolinger, Dwight L. 1940 Word affinities—in Forms of English, ed. by Isamu Abe and Tetsuya Kenekiyo — Cambridge: Harvard University Press (1965) — 191–202.

—— 1950 Rime, assonance, and morpheme analysis —in Forms of English, ed. Isamu Abe and Tetsuya Kenekiyo — Cambridge: Harvard University Press (1965) — 203–26.

Brøndal, Vigo 1939 Linguistique structurale — in Essais de linguistique générale — Copenhagen: (1943) — 90–97.

Cassirer, Ernst 1938 Le concepte de groupe et la théorie de la perception — Journal de psychol. normale et pathologique XXV, 368–414.

—— 1945 Structuralism in Modern Linguistics — Word 1, 99–120.

Chao, Yuen Ren 1954 Review of Jakobson, Fant, Halle, 1952, Preliminaries to Speech Analysis — Romance Philology VIII, 40–46.

Cherry, E. Colin 1956 Roman Jakobson's "Distinctive Features" as the Normal Coordinates of Language — in For Roman Jakobson — The Hague: Mouton — 60–64.

Damourette, J., et E. Pichon 1911–30 Essai de grammaire de la langue française: des mots à la pensee — II — Paris: Editions d'Artrey.

Delas, D. 1973 Phonétique, phonologie et poétique chez R. Jakobson — Langue française 19, 108–19.

Delattre, Pierre 1966 Studies in French and Comparative Phonetics — The Hague: Mouton.

—— 1967 Acoustic or Articulatory Invariance? — Glossa 1:1, 3–25.

—— 1968 From acoustic cues to distinctive features — Phonetica 18, 198–230.

Ducrot, Oswald 1968 Le structuralisme en linguistique — in Qu'est-ce que le structuralisme — Paris: Editions du Seuil.

Ehrenfels, C. 1890 Über Gestaltqualitäten — Vierteljahrsschrift f. wissenschaftliche Philosophie, XIV.

Erlich, Victor 1955 Russian Formalism — The Hague: Mouton.

Fischer-Jørgensen, Eli 1975 Trends in phonological theory — Stockholm: Akademsk Forlag.

Garvin, Paul 1953 Review of Jakobson, Fant, Halle, 1952, Preliminaries to Speech Analysis — Language 29, 472–81.

de George, Richard and Fernande 1972 The structuralists from Marx to Lévi-Strauss — Garden City: Doubleday.

van Ginnekin, Jac. 1956 Roman Jakobson: Pioneer of diachronic phonology — in For Roman Jakobson — The Hague: Mouton — 574–81.

Greenberg, Joseph 1966 Language universals — The Hague: Mouton.

—— (ed.) 1963 Universals of language — Cambridge: MIT Press.

Halle, Morris — In defense of the number two — in Studies presented to Joshua Whatmough — The Hague: Mouton — 65–72.

Holenstein, Elmar 1975a Jakobson and Husserl: contribution to the genealogy of structuralism — The Human Context VII, 61–83.

—— 1974 Jakobson ou le structuralisme phénoménologique — Paris: Seghers (=1975 Roman Jakobsons phänomenologischer Strukturalismus, Frankfurt am Main: Suhrkamp).

—— 1975b Jakobson phénoménologue? — L'Arc 60, 29–37.

Ivić, Pavle 1965 Roman Jakobson and the growth of phonology — Linguistics 18, 35–78.

Joos, Martin 1957 Review of Roman Jakobson and Morris Halle, 1956, Fundamentals of Language — Language 33, 408–15.

Jung, Beat 1973 Saussure–Jakobson, Eine vergleichende Untersuchung über Grundbegriffe der strukturellen Linguistik — Mémoir of the Université Catholique de Louvain.

Karcevskij, S. 1929 Du dualisme asymétrique du signe linguistique — TCLP 1, 88–93.
Krámský, Jiří 1974 The phoneme — München: Fink.
Lane, Michael 1970 Introduction — Introduction to structuralism, ed. by Michael Lane — New York: Basic Books.
Laurent, J-P. 1971 L'analyse de la poésie selon Roman Jakobson — Mémoir of the Université Catholique de Louvain.
Leopold, Werner F. 1956 Roman Jakobson and the study of child language — in For Roman Jakobson — The Hague: Mouton — 285–88.
Lepschy, G. C. 1970 A survey of structural linguistics — London: Faber and Faber.
Lévi-Strauss, Claude 1965 Le triangle culinaire — L'Arc 26, 19–29.
— 1976 Préface to Roman Jakobson, Six leçons sur le son et le sens (1942) — Paris: Edition de Minuit.
Lotz, John 1966 Jakobson's case theory and the Russian prepositions — in To Honor Roman Jakobson — The Hague: Mouton — 1207–12.
Malmberg, Bertil 1970 De Ferdinand de Saussure à Roman Jakobson: L'arbitraire du signe et la substance phonique du langage — Proceedings of the Sixth International Congress of Phonetic Sciences, Prague 1967 — Prague: Academia — 599–603.
Matejka, Ladislav 1975a Crossroads of form and meaning — IJSLP XX, 93–120.
—— 1975b Le formalisme taxonomique et la sémiologie fonctionnelle pragoise — L'Arc 60, 22–28.
Mehta, Ved 1971 John is easy to please — in John is easy to please — Middlesex, England: Penguin — 1974 — (Originally published in the New Yorker, 1971) — 139–188.
Milewski, Th. — De Ferdinand de Saussure à Roman Jakobson: Le progrès de la linguistique en un demi-siècle (1913–1963) — Le Flambeau, No. 3, 1964.
Nattiez, J.-J. 1975 Roman Jakobson dans le siècle — L'Arc 60, 1–2.
Ogden, C. K. 1967 Opposition: A linguistic and psychological analysis — Bloomington, Ind.: Indiana University Press.
Patočka, Jan 1976 Roman Jakobsons phänomenologischer Strukturalismus — Tÿdschrift voor Filosofie 38, 129–35.
Peirce, Charles Sanders 1960 Collected Papers, I–VI — Cambridge: Belknap Press.
Piaget, Jean 1974 Le Structuralisme — 6e édition — Paris: PUP.
Pingaud, Bernard 1965 Comment on devient structuralist? — L'Arc 26, 1–5.
Pos, Hendrik 1938 La notion d'opposition en linguistique — 11e Congrès internationale de psychologie — Paris: Alcan — 246–47.
—— 1939a Phénoménologie et linguistique — Revue internationale de philosophie 1, 354–65.
—— 1939b Perspectives du structuralisme — Etudes phonologiques dédiées à la mémoire de M. le Prince Trubetzkoy — University of Alabama Press, 1964 (=TCLP 8).
Raible, Wolfgang 1974 Roman Jakobson oder "Auf der Wasserscheide zwischen Linguistik und Poetik" — in Roman Jakobson, Aufsätze zur Linguistik und Poetik — München: Nymphenburger Verlagshandlung — 7–37.
Rey, Alain 1974 Une interminable maïeutique — Critique 322, 217–22.
Ruwet, Nicolas 1963 Préface to Roman Jakobson, Essais de linguistique générale (I) — Paris: Editions de Minuit — 7–21.
Sangster, Rodney B. 1970 The linguistic thought of Roman Jakobson — Ph.D. Dissertation — Bloomington: Indiana University.
Sapir, Edward 1921 Language — N.Y.: Harcourt, Brace, World.
Saussure, Ferdinand de 1922 Cours de linguistique générale — Paris: Payot (2e édition).

Scholes, Robert 1974 Structuralism in literature: An introduction — New Haven: Yale University Press.

van Schooneveld, C. H. 1951 The aspect system of the OCS and OR verbum finitum: *byti*. — Word 7, 96–103.

—— 1958 The so-called 'préverbes vides' and neutralization — Dutch contributions to the 4th International Congress of Slavists — The Hague: Mouton — 1–3.

—— 1959 A semantic analysis of the Old Russian finite preterite system — The Hague: Mouton.

—— 1960 On the word order in modern Russian — IJSLP 3, 40–44.

—— 1964 Zur vergleichenden semantischen Struktur der Wortfolge in der russischen, deutschen, französischen und englischen Sprache — Wiener Slavistisches Jahrbuch 2, 94–100.

—— 1967a On the opposition determinate–indeterminate in the contemporary standard Russian verb — American contributions to the 6th International Congress of Slavists 1. — The Hague: Mouton — 351–57.

—— 1976b On the meaning of the Serbocroatian aorist — To honor Roman Jakobson — The Hague: Mouton.

—— 1970 On the morphemic structure of the Slavic word and Greenberg's twenty-eighth universal — The Slavic word, ed. by Dean S. Worth — The Hague: Mouton — 443–48.

—— MS. Semantic transmutations: Prolegomena to a calculus of meaning, I: The cardinal semantic structure of prepositions, cases, and paratactic conjunctions in Contemporary Standard Russian. — In press. — Bloomington, Ind.: Physsardt Publishers.

Shapiro, Maurice 1973 Review of Roman Jakobson, Selected Writings II — Indogermanische Forschungen 78, 193–201.

Silverstein, Michael 1975 La sémiotique jakobsonienne et l'anthropologie sociale — L'Arc 60, 45–49.

Stevens, S. S. 1951 The concept of invariance — Handbook of experimental psychology — New York–London — 19–21.

Thom, René 1974 La linguistique, discipline morphologique exemplaire — Critique 322, 235–45.

Todorov, Tzvetan 1965 Présentation — Théorie de la littérature, ed. T. Todorov — 15–27.

—— 1965 Théorie de la littérature: Textes des formalistes russes — Paris: Seuil.

—— 1971 Roman Jakobson poéticien — Poétique 7, 275–86.

Trnka, Bohumil, *et al* 1958 Prague structural linguistics — in Vachek, A Prague School reader in linguistics — Bloomington, Ind.: Indiana University Press — 468–80.

Vachek, Josef 1966 The linguistic school of Prague — Bloomington: Indiana University Press.

Vallier, Dora 1975 Dans le vif de l'avant-garde — L'Arc 60, 9–13.

Veyrenc, Jacques 1974 Cas et verbe — Critique 322, 246–60.

Waugh, Linda R. 1976a The semantics and paradigmatics of word order — Language 52, 82–107.

—— 1976b Lexical meaning: The prepositions *en* and *dans* in French — Lingua 38, 69–118.

—— 1976c A semantic analysis of the French tense system — Orbis XXIV, 2.

—— 1977 A semantic analysis of word order; Adjective position in French — Leiden: Brill (Cornell Linguistic Contributions) — Preface by Roman Jakobson.

Whitman, Robert 1973 Review of Jakobson, Selected Writings I, Selected Writings II, Bibliography — Language 49, 679–82.

Winner, Thomas 1975 Grands thèmes de la poétique jakobsonienne — L'Arc 60, 55–64.

INDEX

Accusative *see* Case: Russian
Acoustic 26-27, 36, 59n, 76
Acquisition of language *see* Child language acquisition
Active *see* Voice
Agent 28, 40, 71, 82-83
Agreement 34, 100
Alternation 50
Ambiguity 26, 48, 95-96
Analogy 33, 49
Antinomies 16, 23-24, 26, 62, 69
Antonyms 33, 35
Aphasia 15, 34, 85, 89, 91
Aquinas 27
Arbitrariness 17, 44, 46-48, 56, 68-69, 85, 99, 101
Archaic/newfangled 16, 20
Aspect 47, 52, 81, 93
"At" 32, 70, 80, 95, 97
Atomism 22, 54, 101
Attribution 48, 95, 100
Autonomy *see* Relative autonomy

"Bachelor" 35, 72-73
Bally 33
Basic meaning 72, 94, 100; *see also* Grundbedeutung
Baudouin de Courtenay 9
Benveniste 63
Binarism 37, 51, 63, 65-66, 67, 98, 101
Biology 69
Boas 84
Bolinger 46, 97n
Braque 54
Bruner 73
Bubrix 86
Bundling 32-33, 59-60, 62, 75, 78, 78n
"By" 82-84

Case 14, 40-41, 55, 62, 87, 95
  Russian 18-19, 42-44, 46, 48, 52, 55, 60n, 62, 67, 70, 73, 81-84, 93-94
Child language acquisition 15, 49, 64-65, 85, 89, 91
Circularity 24
Clause 16, 22, 35, 60, 86-87
Code 25, 29, 34-35, 74, 101
Code/Message 16, 23-26, 53, 61, 70; *see also individual entries*
Coded matrices 14, 16, 35, 41, 48-49, 56, 61, 86, 98-99
"Colorless green ideas..." 28, 49
Combination *see also* Selection/Combination
  Concurrent 18, 32-36, 59-60, 83, 90
  Sequential 18, 22, 32-36, 96
Communication theory 65
Communicative function 17, 19, 23, 26, 28, 43, 45, 53-55, 61
Commutation 44
Compact/Diffuse 58-59, 66, 71, 78-79, 88, 90
Competence 15, 26
Complementary distribution 76
Complexes 48
Conative function 47; *see also* Functions of language
Concept 38
Conceptual features 43, 59-60, 64n, 80-81, 92-94, 97-98, 99n
Concurrence/Sequence 16; *see also* Combination
Concurrent context *see* Context
Configurative features 43, 45, 50-51
Consonant/Vowel 61, 77-79, 87, 90-91;

see also Vocalic System
Constituent parts 66
Contact 25
Context 18, 22, 25, 31-32, 34-35, 41, 44, 48, 60, 68, 72, 86, 96, 100
Concurrent 45, 57, 59, 72, 76, 78, 85, 90, 97
Sequential 45, 85, 98
Context-Sensitivity 33, 35, 60, 72, 86, 100
Contextual interpretation 31, 37, 68
Contextual meaning 33, 95, 99
Contextual variation 20, 31, 37, 71-72, 74, 83-84, 94, 96; *see also* Invariance/Variation
Contiguity *see* Cimilarity/Contiguity
Contiguity disorders *see* Aphasia
Contingent duality 64
Contrast 59, 64
Creativity 20, 22, 26, 53, 61, 72, 74, 86
Cubism 34, 54
Cultural anthropology 10

Danish dental consonants 76
Dative *see* Case: Russian
Defective phonemes 44
Deixis 24-25, 25n, 63, 99, 99n, 100
Delattre 59n
Demarcative features *see* Configurative features
Denotatum 29; *see also* Reference
Derivation 33, 46
Determinate/Indeterminate 92
Diachrony/Synchrony 16, 20-22, 91
Dialects *see* Sub-codes
Dialectic tension 16, 24, 37, 56
Dialoguical competence 15, 17
Dimensionality 83-84, 93n
Directionality 60n, 67, 73, 83, 93-94
Direct object 82
Discourse 22, 31-32, 35, 60-61, 74, 86
Distinctive/Conceptual 16, 86
Distinctive features *see* Phonological distinctive features
Distribution 18, 44-45, 90, 94
Double articulation 86

Efficiency *see* Relative efficiency
Ehrenfels 62
Einstellung *see* Set
Ellipsis/Explicitness 15-20, 23, 45, 59, 61
Elliptical sub-codes *see* Ellipsis/Explicitness
Emotive function 72; *see also* Functions of language
Emphatic speech 45
Empiricism 27
Encoder/Dedoder 15-16, 24-26, 32-34, 48, 99, 99n
English 20, 25, 29, 29n, 31, 41, 43, 46n, 48, 50-51, 61, 72-73, 80-84, 92-93, 95, 98; *see also* "By" and "At"
/p/ 71
Epic poetry 34
Equivalence/Difference 16, 33-34, 44, 54-55, 67-68, 70-71, 73, 82, 86, 101
Erlich 17, 53
Evening star *see* Morning star
Explicit sub-codes *see* Ellipsis/Explicitness
Expressive features 15, 43, 50-51
Extra-linguistic reality *see* Reference

Features 43; 75; *see also specific types*
Fictitious entities *see* Linguistic fictions
Figurative usage 31, 74, 85, 96; *see also* Metaphor
Fischer-Jörgensen 7n, 65
Flat/Non-flat 58, 76, 91
Folklore 23
Form 40-41, 86
Form/Meaning 32, 42, 45-48, 75, 99; *see also individual entries*
Fortunatov 9
Free/Patterned 16, 61; *see also* Patterning
Free variation 20
French 38-39, 41, 43-44, 66, 71, 77-78, 80-81, 84-85, 91-93; *see also* Vocalic system: French
Frequency 58
Fricative 61
Function 10, 14, 17-18, 26, 41, 43, 45, 59, 71, 86-87; *see also* Teleology
Functions of language 25, 62, 86, 101; *see also individual entries*

Gender 18, 24, 41, 45, 52, 55, 62, 85, 97
General meaning *see* Meaning
Generic 31-33, 37, 39, 72, 80, 95, 99
Genitive *see* Case: Russian
Gesamtbedeutung 31, 94-98
Gestalt psychology 62
Gestaltqualität 17, 60n, 62

Glide 92
Grammar 42, 45, 55-56, 62, 64, 68, 80-85, 92n, 93-94, 98-100
Grammatical categories 18, 24, 62, 71
Grammatical features 35, 44, 59, 67, 75, 88
Grammatical meaning *see* Meaning
Grave/Acute 58, 59n, 66, 71, 79, 88, 90-91
Grundbedeutung 20, 94-98

Hearer *see* Encoder/Decoder
Hierarchical relationships 57, *see also* Hierarchy
Hierarchy 16, 19, 21-22, 35, 51, 53, 56-57, 60-61, 63, 64n, 67, 72, 85-86, 88-89, 96, 98-99, 101
Hierarchy of conceptual features 64n, 99n
Hierarchy of distinctive features 15, 88
Hölderlin 102
Holenstein 7n, 30, 95, 98, 99n
Holes 19, 45
Homogeneity/Individuation 16
Homonymy 19, 33, 41, 46, 48, 75
Husserl 9
Hypostasis 96n

Iconic patterning 87
Iconic symbols *see* Iconicity
Iconicity 34, 39, 47-48, 52
Idiolect 21, 23, 34
Image acoustique 38
Imbalance 18, 45
Implication *see* Mutual implication
Implicational universals 86, 88, 91
Inclusion relation 63, 94, 99n
Independent/Redundant 16; *see also* Redundancy
Indexical symbols *see* Shifters
Inflection 33
Information 41-42, 44, 92
Inherent features 36, 58-59, 64
Inner speech 17, 23, 26
Integration 13-17, 28, 38, 53-54, 61, 99; *see also* Relative autonomy
Intensity 58
Intersyllabic/Intrasyllabic 58
Intrinsic/Contextual 16
Invariance/Variation 8, 16, 63, 72-74, 96, 101; *see also* Relational invariance
Isomorphism 70
Ivić 7n

Juncture 51, 61

Karcevskij 9, 41
Kazan' school 69
Krámský 7n
Kruszewski 9

Language change 18, 20-21, 23, 33, 88
Law-governed 53, 85, 88, 101
Lawful integration 53; *see also* Integration
Levels of structure 21, 22, 41, 53, 56, 63, 66, 86, 100
Lévi-Strauss 9
Lexical features 19, 35, 43, 50, 59, 75
Lexical meaning *see* Meaning
Lexicology 42, 56, 62, 68, 80-85, 92n, 93, 97-100
Linguistic fictions 28, 30, 68, 73, 86, 99
Linguistic imperialism 27
Linguistic reality 15
Linguistic sign 30, 37-53, 56-57, 64, 74-75, 86, 98, 101
  Signans/Signatum 16, 37-53, 68, 99; *see also individual entries*
Linguistic system 10-11, 14-15, 18-19, 21, 27, 29-30, 39, 49, 52, 53-57, 66, 68-69, 73-74, 76, 79, 80n, 81, 98-100, 101
Linguistics 69, 88, 102
Literature 23
Lyric poetry 34

Malmberg 7n
Marginality 42, 60n, 83-84, 93-94
Markedness 37, 67, 89-100, 101
  Marked/Unmarked 16, 21, 35, 37, 68, 93, 99-100
  Markedness assimilation 98
  Markedness reversals 87, 98
  Non-accumulation of marks 91, 97-98
  Unmarked term 89, 94-97
  Unmarked meaning *see* Zero meaning
Matejka 7n, 13n
Material entity *see* Non-material nature of language
Mathematics 69
Matrices *see* Coded matrices
Meaning 28-32, 39, 41-42, 44, 49, 62, 94-98, 99n

Basic meaning 72, 94, 100; *see also* Grundbedeutung
General meaning 32, 34, 73-74, 94-99
Lexical meaning/Grammatical meaning 16, 55, 72, 84, 86, 100
Peripheral meaning 20, 100; *see also* Contextual variation
Syntactic meaning 49
Unmarked meaning *see* Zero meaning
Means-ends view of language *see* Teleology
Mere otherness 43-45, 51, 75
Message 25, 34-35, 60, 101
Metalinguistic function 24, 33; *see also* Functions of language
Metaphor/Metonymy 16, 22, 33-34, 74, 96
Methodology 9n, 14, 46, 54, 70; 75
Milewski 7n
Modification 71, 95
Monod 30
Mood 24
Morning star 28-29
Morpheme 14, 33, 44, 50, 58, 60, 60n
Morphology 16, 19, 42, 62
Morphonology 50
Moscow school 9
Multi-layering 60
Mutability 21
Mutual implication 37, 53, 63, 64n, 65, 67, 97, 101

Narrated event 16, 24, 32, 63; *see also* Reference
Nasal/Oral 58, 79-80, 88, 90-91
Natural language 14
Near-universals 85-86, 91
Neurophysiology 73
Neutralization 44, 89, 91; *see also* Defective phonemes
Nominal/Verbal 43, 51, 62, 84, 87
Nominative *see* Case
Non-material nature of language 17, 22, 26, 28, 53
Novel contexts 22, 61, 72; *see also* Creativity
Nullbedeutung *see* Zero meaning
Number 18, 39, 41, 47, 52, 55, 87, 93, 97

Obligatory category 84
Observer 99n
One form-one meaning principle 46, 75
Onomatopoeia 46
Ontological reality *see* Reference
Opposition 37, 39, 44, 63-68, 76-77, 86, 88-89, 101
Oppositional component 66
Overal/Contextual 16
Overlapping 24

Paradigmatic 32-33, 35, 44, 53-54, 86
Paradigmatic Set *see* Substitution set
Part/Whole 11, 14, 49, 56-63, 69, 75, 78n, 94
Particular/Universal 16; *see also* Universal invariance
Parts of speech 51n, 62, 84
Passive *see* Voice
Patterning 15, 18, 33, 49, 62, 85, 87, 99
Peirce 9, 24, 39, 46-47
Percept/Concept 99
Perception 15, 19, 26, 59, 64, 73, 81, 99, 99n
Person 24, 41, 52
Personal pronouns 32, 66, 94
Phenomenology 9
Phoneme 17, 26-27, 31-32, 35, 42-43, 49, 54, 57-58, 60, 66, 70-71, 73, 75, 77, 98
Phoneme combinations 51-52
Phonemic system 14-15, 65
Phonesthemes 46
Phonetics 27, 55, 68
Phonological distinctive features 15, 20, 26-27, 33, 35, 42-43, 45, 57, 60, 72, 75-80, 88, 90-92, 98-99
Phonology 15-16, 26, 42-43, 56, 64, 75-80, 90-92, 92n, 97-100
Phrase 16, 22, 32, 35, 60, 86
Physics 69
Pichon 85
Pidgins and creoles 22
Plural *see* Number
Poetic function 14, 22, 26, 31, 72, 74; *see also* Functions of language
Pointing 30, 39-40
Pos 37, 64
Predictability 65, 67
Predication 33, 35, 48, 93, 95, 100
Prepositions 41, 48-49, 62, 70-71, 81-84, 95

Principles of organization 7-11, 16, 21-22, 101
Processes 10
Productivity 20-21, 26, 74
Proper names 24, 31, 52, 64
Proportions 70
Prosodic features 36, 58, 64
Psychology 10, 62

Quantification 83, 94

Raible 7n
Realism 34
Redundancy 19-20, 43, 45, 53, 71, 92, 100
Redundant features 15, 43, 45, 59
Reference 28-31, 39, 49, 68, 69n, 80, 99; *see also* World of human experience
Referential function 25, 47; *see also* Functions of language
Relational invariance 37, 46, 67-88, 99, 101; *see also* Invariance/Variation
Relational properties 69
Relations 24, 37, 42, 53-56, 69, 77, 86, 101
Relative autonomy 13-16, 26, 42, 45, 53, 61, 89, 98, 101
Relative efficiency 18-20, 53, 64-65
Rey 7n
Rhetoric 31
Romanticism 34
Russian 18, 29n, 51, 72-73, 81-82, 85, 92-94, 96-97; *see also* Case: Russian Palatalized dentals 15, 89

Sangster 74
Sapir 84
Saussure 9, 21, 23, 33, 38, 46, 66
Schizophrenia 102
Sechehaye 9
Secondary motivation 46
Selection/Combination 16, 32-36, 49, 51-52, 60n, 100-101
Semantic system 25, 35, 41, 42n
Semiotics 10, 17, 23, 26-27, 30, 38-39, 55-56, 68-69
Sentence level 16, 22, 32, 35, 48-49, 51, 60, 86, 100
Set 25, 62
Sexuisemblance 85
Sharp/Plain 72
Shifters 24, 32, 34, 48, 52
"Shooting of the hunters" 95
Sign *see* Linguistic sign
Signans 38-53, 59, 64, 74-80, 101; *see also* Linguistic sign *and* Zero signans
Signatum 29, 38-53, 65, 74, 80-85, 92-94, 101; *see also* Linguistic sign *and* Zero signatum
Signifiant *see* Signans
Signification 42-43, 45, 62, 99
Signifié *see* Signatum
Similarity/Contiguity 16, 32-36, 47-48, 64, 74, 96
Similarity disorder *see* Aphasia
Simplicity 19; *see also* Relative efficiency
Singular/Plural *see* Number
Social dialects 23
Sociology 10
Sound 17, 26-28, 37-38, 68; *see also* Speech sound
Spatial dialects 23
Spatial dynamism 22
Speaker *see* Encoder/Decoder
Speech event 16, 24-26, 48, 63, 96
Speech sounds 27-32, 37, 39, 59, 59n, 73, 99
Sprachbund 22
Statics/Dynamics 16, 20-23, 101
Stevens 59n
Stridency 58, 79, 90
Structural laws 23, 57, 88, 98
Structuralism 9-10
Structure 13-14, 17, 21-22, 25, 32, 37, 53-56, 86, 88, 99, 101; *see also* Linguistic system
Stylistic variation 20-21, 72, 74, 97
Sub-codes 21, 23, 26, 61
Subject 47, 49, 71, 86-87, 93, 95-96
Substitution 33, 35, 42
Substitution set 33, 35-36, 44
Surrealism 34
Sweet 80
Syllable 18, 22, 60, 60n, 86-87, 89
Symbol 31, 46-47
Symbolism 34
Syncretism 33, 46n, 52, 91-92, 97
Scission 91, 91n
Synesthesia 43, 46
Synonymy 33, 35, 39, 43-44
Syntactic matrices *see* Coded matrices
Syntactic meaning *see* Meaning
Syntagmatic 32-33, 48, 56

Syntax 16, 18, 35, 42, 62, 71, 96, 99-100
System *see* Linguistic system
System of signs 30, 49, 56-57

Teilganzes 56; *see also* Part/Whole
Teleology 17-18, 26-27, 39, 53, 101
Tense 24, 41, 52, 66, 71, 80-81, 84, 89, 96-97
Tense/Lax 58, 77-78, 80
Theory of relativity 69
Time 58
Topology 69
Transfer 17, 39, 96
Translation 33, 39
Triple phonological triangles 90
Trubetzkoy 9
Tynjanov 53
Typology 21, 41, 65, 87, 99

Ultimate constituents 57, 98
Units 14, 27, 33, 37, 42, 49, 51-52, 54, 56, 59-60, 66, 69, 86
Universal tendencies 86; *see also* Near-universals
Universal invariance 85-88; *see also* Implicational universals
Unmarked meaning *see* Zero meaning
Unmarked term *see* Markedness
Utterance 22, 35, 60, 86

Vagueness 95, 99
van Schooneveld 7n, 9, 25n, 46n, 64n, 70, 80n, 84, 93, 94n, 99n
Variation *see* Invariance/Variation
Verbal *see* Nominal/Verbal
Vocabulary 42-43, 64, 100
Vocalic system *see also* Consonant/Vowel
  French 21, 77, 89
  Gilyak 77
Voice 19, 28, 39, 45, 52, 71, 80, 93
Vowel *see* Consonant/Vowel

Waugh 66, 71, 84, 93
Whitman 101
Word 16, 18, 33, 35, 44, 49, 51, 51n, 59-61, 75, 86, 100
Word order 41, 47, 86-87, 93
World of human experience 24, 30, 37-39, 43, 63, 69n, 84, 99
Written language 14, 17, 40

Zero meaning 41, 92; *see also* Markedness
Zero phoneme 92
Zero property 90n, 92n
Zero quality *see* Zero property
Zero signans 40, 42, 52, 87
Zero Signatum 42

1) Gathers together & synthesizes vast range of [illegible] purely linguistic theorizing.

2) Like [illegible]'s own writing often too terse, compact to be comprehensible w/o solid background
esp on examples – cf 51
graciously written

3) Requires familiarity w/ linguistic theory
general linguistic

Upper Division courses in linguistics
" " philosophy

Contrast w/ Hjelmslev
short on examples